# BLOW YOUR MIND

Kristian Steenstrup

Blow Your Mind
By Kristian Steenstrup
© Kristian Steenstrup and
The Royal Academy of Music, Aarhus

ISBN 978-87-989022-2-5

Copy-editing: Laura Garwin
Layout: Stine Sandahl. www.sandahls.net
Printed by Graphicunit

The Royal Academy of Music, Aarhus/
Det Jyske Musikkonservatorium

http://www. musikkons.dk

Please feel free to contact the author for
comments or questions at krs@musikkons.dk

# BLOW YOUR MIND

Kristian Steenstrup

# TABLE OF CONTENTS

**INTRODUCTION** ........................................................................... 8
**SONG AND WIND** ...................................................................... 11
    Music entering and leaving the brain ........................... 11
    The acoustics of brass instruments ............................... 13
    Growing the voice in the head ........................................ 15
**PITCH, DURATION, LOUDNESS AND TIMBRE** ................. 19
    **Pitch** ........................................................................................ 21
        Singing and solmization ................................................ 21
        Mouthpiece playing ....................................................... 22
        Intonation ......................................................................... 24
        Playing with others ........................................................ 25
        Playing with a drone ..................................................... 26
    **Duration** ................................................................................. 27
    **Loudness** ............................................................................... 28
    **Timbre** ................................................................................... 30
**FOCUSING ON THE SONG** .................................................... 33
**THE EMBOUCHURE** ................................................................ 37
    Free buzzing ......................................................................... 41
    The rim .................................................................................... 42
    Sensing the vibrating surface ......................................... 43
    Contact pressure ................................................................ 43
    High range ............................................................................ 43
**BREATHING** ............................................................................... 46
    Physiology of breathing ................................................... 47
    Posture .................................................................................... 50
    Psychology of breathing .................................................. 53
        Inhalation .......................................................................... 54
        Exhalation ........................................................................ 56
        H-consonants ................................................................. 58

| | |
|---|---|
| **Breathing equipment** | **59** |
| The Breath Builder | 60 |
| The Breathing Bag | 61 |
| The Incentive Spirometer | 61 |
| The Variable Resistance Compound Gauge | 62 |
| **Breathing exercises** | **62** |
| **THE TONGUE** | **64** |
| **The consonant** | **65** |
| **The illusion of staccato** | **66** |
| **The vowel** | **67** |
| Using the Venturi effect | 71 |
| **ZEN AND THE ART OF EMBOUCHURE MAINTENANCE** | **72** |
| **PRACTICING** | **76** |
| **A myelin concerto** | **77** |
| **Neurons that fire together, wire together** | **80** |
| **Slow practice** | **81** |
| **The Flow Zone** | **82** |
| **Deliberate practice** | **84** |
| **Structuring practice time** | **87** |
| Blocked practice | 88 |
| Random practice | 88 |
| Varied practice | 91 |
| **Learning styles** | **93** |
| **Mental practice** | **95** |
| **Brain waves and performance** | **97** |
| Centering | 101 |
| Practicing centering | 104 |

## INTRODUCTION

Nearly a decade has passed since the publication of the second edition of *Teaching Brass* (2007), which was based on the first edition published in 2004. My motivation for writing that book was the feeling that, at that time, there was not much literature available that attempted to deal thoroughly with scientific aspects of brass playing—particularly in the context of the pedagogy of Arnold Jacobs (1915–1998), as compared with other schools of thought.

Arnold Jacobs, who was the tuba player of the Chicago Symphony for more than 40 years, spent most of his life investigating what knowledge could be gleaned from natural sciences such as anatomy, acoustics, respiratory physiology, neurology and psychology (to name just a few) about the workings of a healthy brass musician. Having accumulated this knowledge, he used it to develop a different approach to brass playing than was usual at the time.

Jacobs had a tremendous influence on several generations of brass players, especially in the United States, and gained a reputation as one of the most influential brass teachers of all time. During his lifetime he challenged a lot of the dogma surrounding brass and wind methodologies, but unfortunately he never wrote a book about his ideas. I was fortunate enough to have been taught by Jacobs during the last nine years of his life, so, at the beginning of the 21$^{st}$ century, with his ideas just beginning to spread to Europe and other parts of the world, I felt it was important to communicate some of these ideas in a form that would be useful to brass teachers, supported by scientific information and accompanied by a critical assessment of the competing schools of thought. In the intervening years, many of Jacobs' concepts—in particular, the physiological aspects of his teachings—have become more widely accepted, and have had a significant effect on brass pedagogy.

As its title implies, the present book focuses more on the mental aspects of brass playing and performance. In the past decade or so, an abundance of literature dealing with psychological and neurological aspects of music performance has appeared, confirming some earlier ideas that were often based on empirical knowledge, rather than systematic research. To further enhance learning for future generations, I find it imperative to convey some of these findings in a practical, written form for brass players.

This book also deals with physiological aspects of brass playing, but in far less detail than was the case in *Teaching Brass*. Readers who would like to learn more about these matters are encouraged to refer to that book.

# SONG AND WIND

## Music entering and leaving the brain

When we listen to music—whether we are trained musicians with highly developed, discriminating ears, or laypeople simply enjoying the beauty of the sounds and the emotions they awake—a fascinating transformation of energy takes place at the moment the sound leaves the instruments or loudspeakers and enters our ears and brains. In physics, music is merely a collection of sound waves, propagated by the vibrations of air molecules. But in psychology, when music is perceived in the brain of a listener, it's the sensation and meaning of the sounds that matter.

Music travels through the air as waves of compression and expansion. These sound waves are sensed by hair cells in the inner ear, which bend in response to vibrations in the surrounding fluid. The hairs are organized in such a way as to be sensitive to particular vibration frequencies, according to their position along the length of the snail-shaped cochlea. Thus, the hair cells near the beginning of the cochlea respond preferentially to high-pitched sounds, while those near the end respond to lower pitches.[1] When the hair cells bend, they cause an electrical signal to be sent through the auditory nerve, to the auditory cortex of the brain. Here, finally, is where we perceive the sound and start to make sense of what we hear, while we begin to engage other parts of the brain to facilitate the decoding process. Neuroscientists do not yet understand why the firing of neurons gives rise to experience and mental engagement, such as thinking; nevertheless, they can see that when certain regions of the brain are active, we tend to have particular types of experience, associated with those regions. It's fascinating how, when we listen to music, what starts as mechanical energy (sound waves) is converted to electrical energy (nerve impulses), and is then translated into perception, the experience of music.

When we perform music, we have to carry out a similar task in reverse order: we must conceive music—have a strong mental idea of what

---

1  Jourdain, Robert. *Music, the Brain, and Ecstasy* (Avon Books, 1997).

we want to perform—and then translate this psychological energy into electrical signals travelling down motor nerves to the muscle groups responsible for controlling whatever instrument we are attempting to play. A vocalist has to mentally conceive and hear a tone, engage the auditory cortex in the recollection of the particular note, and engage the nerves in sending signals to the different parts of the body responsible for performing this task. Vocal cords have to be given information about what tension they need to assume, in order to vibrate the precise number of times per second to hit the right note; expiratory muscle groups need to be told exactly how to contract, in order to generate the appropriate airflow and pressure at the vocal cords so they can vibrate; and the tongue needs to know its position for the consonant and vowel of the particular word. The electrical energy carrying this information is now made into vibration, creating sound waves that will leave the singer's mouth and travel to the listener, whose brain, one hopes, will translate the vibrations into beautiful music. Almost miraculously, the accomplished singer needs only to think of the desired output, conceive in his mind its creation, and be able to trust his body while the coordination and organization of the different muscle groups involved are handled subconsciously.

There are many similarities between singing and brass playing. Like singers, we brass players have to vibrate pieces of flesh—in our case, not vocal cords, but lips—and we have to engage the breathing apparatus to supply appropriate air power at the source of vibration. We also have to use the tongue to articulate.

When we think of a singer conceiving the music, in order to "tell the vocal cords what to do", it seems obvious that this is absolutely necessary. Popularly, this has been referred to as "having the notes in the ear" before singing the first note, and knowing the melody, the order of the notes. Today, we naturally refer to this as "hearing the music in the mind"—more precisely, the brain, or even more specifically, the auditory cortex. As brass playing is so analogous to singing, it is of vital importance that we communicate to our structures—especially to our lips, the brass player's vocal cords—in much the same manner. Arnold Jacobs used to describe in lectures how the brain of the successful brass player is similarly wired to that of a singer, with the neurological difference being that, whereas the singer activates the tenth cranial nerve, the vagus nerve, with its branches to the larynx, the brass player fires the seventh cranial nerve, the facial nerve, which supplies the lips. But initially, as the order is carried out by the brain at the level of thought, these two types of musician are very much alike.

Surprisingly, though, when we look at method books for brass players or surf the Web for guidance, it becomes clear that this essential facet of controlling a brass player's physiology is very often neglected. Brass players seem very much occupied with the mechanical and physiological aspects of playing, which of course have their complications, but which also do not make much sense if the musical aspects are not cared for.

So often, when a brass student is struggling with a difficult passage, it appears that he or she is not really "singing" the music mentally, but trying to control the muscles directly, often with strong frustration. By contrast, when brass players start to sing the correct pitches and rhythms while playing, their success rates immediately improve.

## The acoustics of brass instruments

Intuitively, brass instruments seem closely related to woodwind instruments, and of course both belong to the larger group of "wind" instruments. When it comes to basic tone production, there are a number of similarities. All wind players excite the air column inside a tube by vibrating a reed, a double reed or their lips. Flutists use an "air reed", which excites vibration of the flute's air column when the player's airstream hits the edge of the embouchure hole. The key for all wind instruments is getting the air to vibrate inside a tube of varying length, even though the way the vibration is generated varies widely among the different groups.[2]

The air column inside any wind instrument will vibrate at a pitch determined by its length. In an ideal cylindrical pipe, open at both ends, the air column can vibrate at its fundamental frequency and integer multiples of this frequency, according to the harmonic series (octave, fifth, second octave, major third, minor third, even smaller minor third, third octave, and so on). Modern brass instruments are designed to be able to reproduce this harmonic series, which for an instrument in C corresponds to C, C, G, C, E, G, Bb, C, etc..

Woodwind instruments play close to the fundamental pitch of the tube when all of the instrument's holes are closed, and players shorten the length of the air column (to play chromatically) by opening holes with the fingers. This means that players are always playing near the bottom of the harmonic series, where there is a large distance between the

---

[2] Often wind players are not aware of the fact that their sound comes from the air column inside the instrument, rather than from the material of which it is made. The instrument vibrates very little, and therefore does not contribute as much to the sound as intuition might suggest. The internal geometry of the instrument determines the form and shape of the air column and this has a big influence, but it can be difficult to know exactly what the instrument maker has done here, since it is not readily visible. As for the material used, the most important factor is how much of the vibration created by the player is lost to wall vibration and friction inside the tube. It seems that the material must have a certain stiffness to avoid too much wall vibration and consequent loss of air vibration energy, but whether an expensive material such as gold is better in this regard than cheaper materials is currently debated. How much placebo effect might there be in choosing an expensive instrument, with a lot of gold, which is also endorsed by our favorite, amazing player of that instrument? It is interesting that it is now possible to create quite good instruments made of plastic, for a fraction of the price of conventional instruments. A test of seven otherwise identical Muramatsu flutes, made from materials ranging from 24 karat gold to silver-coated alloy yielded this interesting conclusion: "Tests with experienced professional flutists and listeners and one model of a flute made by Muramatsu from 7 different materials showed no evidence that the wall material has any appreciable effect on the sound color or dynamic range of the instrument." [Linortner, Renate. Silver, Gold, Platinum – and the Sound of the Flute (2001). https://iwk.mdw.ac.at/?page_id=97.]
A similar study of trombones yielded parallel results, in that none of the professional trombonists recruited by Richard Smith could distinguish different types or thicknesses of material in the bell of the trombone. Smith, R. The effect of material in brass instruments: a review. *Proceedings of The Institute of Acoustics* **8**, 91-96 (1986).

possible tones that can resonate in the air column. This effect "enslaves" the reed, allowing the player to play only the permitted note for any fingering. This gives great security to the player; indeed, it is rare to hear woodwind players miss notes to anything near the extent we hear on brass instruments.

By contrast, brass players, and especially French horn players, often play much higher in the harmonic series—a state of affairs that was even more extreme before the invention of valves, when one needed to be very high up in the harmonic series to play diatonically or chromatically. (The exception, of course, were sackbut players, who could change the length of their instruments with a slide, as trombone players do today.) The addition of valves to brass instruments allows the tube to be lengthened progressively by semitones, so that we are playing on seven different natural horns, each with its own harmonic overtone series. This allows us to play chromatically, even in the lowest range of the instrument.

Because they play higher in the harmonic series, where the notes are closer together, brass players need to have a fine control over the lips' vibration frequency, which very much determines what note comes out of the instrument. The vibration of the lips also determines whether the pitch will be close to the most resonant point (the "tone center") of the instrument for the note that's being played, allowing the player to play with a "great sound". As we control this fundamental aspect of playing with our lips and the constant changing of their geometry and degree of tension or stiffness, we resemble singers, the only other musicians who produce the initial vibration in tone production with meat, rather than an inanimate material such as a string, a reed or a drum.

## Growing the voice in the head

Arnold Jacobs encapsulated the similarity of playing a brass instrument to the act of singing with the educational concept, "Song and Wind". "Song" must be present in the mind, in the auditory cortex that will tell the lips how to vibrate—with what frequency, amplitude and duration. Furthermore, by mentally hearing the desired articulation as part of the "song", rather than by conscious manipulation of muscles, the brass player is also able to control the tongue. Likewise, by thinking "wind"—air in movement at the lips—the player's airstream from the lungs becomes the motor force of vibration. We will get back to wind and tongue later, after first discussing aspects pertaining to song, the initial musical thought in the brass player's brain.

Song, for the brass player, can mean the aural image: the desired sound of the instrument playing the music in question, including all musical aspects such as tone color, pitch, dynamics and vibrato. The stronger this mental image, the clearer will be the message sent to the physical structures involved in playing. Song could also be listening to and imitating a better player—actually hearing him or her mentally while playing—or it could be hearing one's own voice in one's mind while performing. Listening to musicians of all types, and imitating their musicianship—and, especially, trying to emulate great singers—are wonderful ways of learning phrasing and expression. The brass player imagining the singing of Maria Callas or Luciano Pavarotti will initiate a strong musical stimulus. There is no one right way to build helpful mental images; players are individuals, and react in their own ways to different methods for engaging in mental singing.

Imitation—in which a student hears his teacher play a passage, and directly afterwards tries to emulate the playing—is a powerful way of programming the mind to focus on the desired output, the musical "product". The idea is to let the brain subconsciously organize the muscles responsible for producing the output, as an alternative to verbal instruction, in which the teacher tries to explain exactly what to do. A student can also listen to recordings of great players, which are available in great abundance, and have never been easier or more affordable to obtain. Beyond listening to general aspects of a superior musician's playing, when a student is hoping to acquire a specific virtue, she can flood her brain with the sound of the role model's playing. For example, if a trumpet player wants to study vibrato and know the different ways to use it, he can listen to recordings of players who illustrate very different styles of vibrato. Timofei Dokshizer's vibrato is quite different from Maurice André's, not to mention that of an orchestral player such as Adolph Herseth. There is no one right way, but many possibilities, according to style, period, mood and so forth, and it is an advantage for the young player to learn these different ways of applying vibrato, as with timbre, articulation and countless other virtues. The student can listen to a few bars of a recording of a piece that she is playing, then press pause and try to sound exactly like the recording, and keep repeating the short section until success has been obtained. When a student constantly compares his own playing with that of a worldclass player of the same instrument, it gives repeated opportunities for fruitful discrimination between great and merely adequate playing. Pretty soon, the desired sound will start to override one's own sound, and a strong aural image will form.[3]

A great way to learn to sing in the brain while playing a brass instrument is to learn to sing with the voice. When singing with the voice, we can really monitor and determine whether the music is strongly programmed into the mind. One does not have to sing with a great operatic voice, although when students start to engage the voice and practice singing regularly, it usually improves. Singing is probably the earliest way of making music in our evolutionary history, and we often admire players who have the ability to play their instrument as an extension of the human voice. Through singing, we can establish pitch, rhythm, phrasing, vibrato and dynamics; and although breathing and aerodynamic conditions for the brass player are quite different from those for a singer, even here there are some similarities, such as the ability to sing or play without excessive tension. If we first learn the music by singing, then, when we pick up the instrument, we are not asking a question of the

---

[3] There can be some problems with listening to trumpets in an orchestra (whether live or on a recording), and even with listening to a teacher playing to the student. In the orchestra, trumpets have a more soprano sound than they do at close range, because some of the lower harmonics of the trumpet sound will be covered by lower instruments, such as trombones, horns, bassoons and lower strings. Also, a trumpet will sound much more brilliant from in front of the bell, because higher frequencies are more directional than lower frequencies, which spread more broadly. This is why a subwoofer in a stereo or surround-sound system can be placed almost anywhere in the room, but the tweeter most often points directly at the listener. The sound that the player hears from her playing position behind the bell is therefore much rounder that what is heard in front. If the student tries to emulate the sound heard from the front of someone else's bell, either as played directly towards him or when listening to recordings with the microphone placed similarly, the student's sound may be too bright. It is better for the teacher to stand next to the student, so the student will hear what the teacher hears when he or she plays.

lips or the metal, but instead, with conviction and authority, we are telling our musical story, putting the correct vibrations into the tube in cooperation with its interior air column, which has no other choice than to resonate. When brass players cannot sing what they are trying to play, it is most often more difficult for them to play, even with the help from the instrument.

Song in the brain has its effect on instrumental playing through outgoing messages transmitted by the facial nerve, also known as the seventh cranial nerve. This motor nerve, which controls the muscles of facial expression, carries instructions to guide the lips, note by note, to assume the configuration necessary to create the desired pitches, in cooperation with the flow of air from the lungs exciting the air column of the instrument. The excellent brass player has a strong musical story to tell, incorporating excitement and other emotions in the music. The outgoing messages are important, but human beings are also equipped with sensory nerves, sending messages back to the brain for evaluation. We have sensory awareness of how we sound, and also of how we feel in the body—and especially in the lips, one of the most sensitive areas of our anatomy. This sensory awareness can sometimes be overemphasized, so that a player starts to try to play by feel, particularly in the lips, and by listening to herself. Listening to ourselves gives us great feedback about what we just did, but it does not necessarily help in telling the lips what to do to sound great on the next note. The fifth cranial nerve (the trigeminal nerve), which is in part sensory, sends messages back to the brain about how hard we are working, how tired we are, whether our lips are wet or dry, and so forth—information that is often not going to have much influence on the outward message except as a distraction. The sensory and motor pathways are like one-way streets, sending information in opposite directions, and the really great brass players have an amazing ability to let the outgoing message dominate, while partially ignoring the incoming message. Is our aural image of the music we are playing—the song—so strong that even if we are not feeling our best, the signals travelling down the facial nerve keep going? Or do we react to the poor feeling by analyzing and becoming introverted?

The worse we feel, the stronger the song must be. Learning to play a brass instrument is to grow the voice in the head.

## PITCH, DURATION, LOUDNESS AND TIMBRE

Growing the voice in the head is a huge task, with a difficulty that varies according to the individual. Some students have been exposed to a lot of musical programming during their childhoods. Their parents may be musicians, they may have done much singing or playing from an early age, or they may have heard a lot of high-quality music. The age at which children begin to take music lessons regularly, or play in an ensemble, and how much time is spent practicing and the quality of that practice varies widely. This variation in early experience, leads to a large variation in musical abilities among students.

Traditionally, musical talent[4] has been viewed as something genetic, something inborn and inherited, but more and more research is showing that "talent" has more to do with learning, especially the quantity and quality of practice. We are not born to play brass instruments, but— as we shall see later in the chapter about practicing—as we spend a lot of time with the challenges of mastering the instrument, doing what has become known as "deliberate practice", the brain develops mental representations of the particular task. The resulting facility comes from connections between neurons being established and strengthened during practice, rather than being an ability that is pre-programmed from birth. In other words, talent is not born but *grown*, in response to what we have been doing for thousands of hours.[5][6][7] Modern pedagogy is moving away from categorizing students as talented or not, and towards finding methods to motivate and improve a student's musicianship in the most resourceful way. One effective way of educating a young student towards the complex abilities of a fully trained musician is to break a seemingly tremendous task into smaller units, each of which is eminently achievable.

---

[4] Hansen, Niels Christian. New perspectives on the study of musical expertise. *Danish Musicology Online, special Issue on Music and Brain Research* (2015).
[5] Ericsson, Anders and Pool, Robert. *Peak: Secrets from the New Science of Expertise* (Houghton Mifflin Harcourt, 2016).
[6] Colvin, Geoff. *Talent is Overrated: What Really Separates World-Class Performers from Everybody Else* (Nicholas Brealy Publishing, 2008).
[7] Sloboda, John A. et al. The role of practice in the development of performing musicians. *British Journal of Psychology* **87**, 287-309 (1996).

As described in the first chapter, our ability to make sense of music relies on the processing of musical sound in the brain's auditory cortex. According to music psychologists[8], this starts with decoding the sound into four parameters: pitch, duration, loudness and timbre. Pitch is determined by the vibration frequency—for example, 440 vibrations per second in the US and UK, and 442 in continental Europe (in the EU, we are sharper!) for an orchestra's tuning A. Duration encompasses anything having to do with time, or rhythm. Loudness—more often referred to in the musical context as dynamic level, or "dynamics"— is measured in decibels. Timbre has to do with the spectrum of harmonic overtones to a given fundamental: the amplitudes of the different possible overtones determine the type of sound that we hear. Thus, for example, an oboe has a charateristic pattern of harmonics that is different from those of a flute. Beyond this, a sensitive ear (and brain) can discern personal variations among diverse instrumentalists on an identical instrument, and an individual musician can change the color of his instrument's sound, according to the mood he wants to express.

Although it may sound like an oversimplification, everything we hear in music is based on a combination of these four basic parameters. For example, vibrato is a combination of pitch fluctuations (narrow or wider) and time (faster or slower). Phrasing can be described as small changes in dynamics (loudness)—so, for example, the high point of the phrase may be the loudest. Phrasing can also come from changes in the intensity of vibrato, or from changes in the time dimension, such as increasing the tempo slightly towards a climax. Another complex feature of music, harmonic structure, is a combination of pitch and time. Even the emotional effect on listeners of an artist like Maria Callas can be traced to a certain timbre in her voice, which she was able to deploy along with time, dynamics and pitch to move her audience. Thus, the possible combinations of the four basic virtues are endless, and endlessly rich. We are not born with great musicianship, but we can begin to establish it by studying and implementing these basic aural skills.

---

8    Seashore, Carl E. *Psychology of Music* (McGraw Hill, 1938).

## Pitch

As discussed earlier, the nature of brass instruments requires their players to have precise control over the vibration frequency (and hence the pitch) generated by their buzzing lips, in order to excite the desired note in the instrument's air column. If a pianist has poor pitch recognition or recall, it may not be a serious problem, as the pitches are built into the instrument. But for brass players, whose instruments supply only the potential to resonate with a vibration supplied by the lips, it is essential to be able to hear a desired pitch before playing it.

### *Singing and solmization*

One of the best ways to develop an inner sense of pitch is by singing a lot, and in tune. Make a rule that you must be able to sing everything that you are going to play correctly and in tune. Keep a pitch source—such as a piano—close to you when you are singing, so that you can keep checking whether you are singing the correct pitches of the music being rehearsed.[9] An even more efficient way to internalize pitch is by the practice of solfège, or, more precisely, solmization—a system of assigning a specific syllable to each note of the musical scale. Any consistent set of names for the notes will work, but you might as well use the Italian names, as they flow very easily and are already widely used in the Western world. These are Do, Re, Mi, Fa, So, La, Ti, Do, for a C-major scale. It may seem odd to do this, instead of just singing the notes, but this centuries-old tradition has a reason: it strengthens the connection in the brain between written music and the pitches and rhythms that it represents, as 'heard' in the mind. This reflects a principle in neuroscience that underlies all learning: "Neurons that fire together, wire together." This means that when neurons that are responsible for one mental task, or physical skill, are activated at the same time as neurons in charge of another task or skill, these two different groups of neurons start to make connections with each other. When we repeatedly think of and sing the note named Do, the neurons responsible for conceiving or mentally hearing the pitch C become activated. In other words, the use of syllables in solmization strengthens the relationship to the pitch they represent.

---

[9] For the smartphone generation, it is easy to have a pitch source always handy, in the form of countless apps that will provide tones as desired.

The two main ways of using solmization in the Western world are the "fixed-Do" and "moveable-Do" systems. In fixed-Do, Do always represents C, Re always D, and so on. In moveable-Do, Do is the tonic in whatever key is being played. So, in C-major, Do will be C, but in F-major, Do will be F. Fixed-Do is a great way of relating absolute pitches to the written notes, whereas moveable-Do helps a player to develop a sense of tonality, harmonic progression and each note's role in a given key. There seems to be a greater overall value in practicing moveable-Do, but it is also more complex and time-consuming, as the student must continually analyze the music's harmonic structure, to be able to choose the correct key. This can be very difficult, or even impossible, in late-Romantic and 20$^{th}$-century music.

In my experience, most students can quickly learn and benefit from practicing fixed-Do solmization, whereas it takes a lot of time and effort before moveable-Do can be used in the brass player's repertoire. Fixed-Do is also more widespread, having long been incorporated into the educational systems of countries such as Italy, France, Belgium, Spain, the countries of Eastern Europe, and Japan. By contrast, the moveable-Do system, having originated in Hungary as part of the Kodaly system, spread to other countries somewhat later. Hungarians have traditionally learned both systems from early childhood, and I am sure this is one of the reasons why Hungarian brass players are doing so well in the music world of today. Learning both systems would be ideal, but one has to be realistic when trying to persuade students from Northern Europe, with very limited solmization skills, to take up such a practice.

Arnold Jacobs recommended Pasquale Bona's book, *Rhythmical Articulation*, as an excellent book for solfège. It is easy in the beginning, and it progresses so smoothly that the challenges grow very gradually. After only a few days, the student will feel that she has made progress, but the practice must be kept up for years—depending, of course, on the student's individual progress.

### Mouthpiece playing
Another great way for brass players to improve their sense of pitch is to play the mouthpiece, when it is not attached to the instrument. Sometimes teachers discourage students from doing this, as the physical process and degree of effort are somewhat different from those of playing the

complete instrument. As we've seen, when the mouthpiece is attached to the instrument, buzzing in the mouthpiece cup excites resonances in the instrument's air column according to the harmonics allowed by the tube length, as determined by the valve combination or slide position. The same principle applies when playing the mouthpiece alone, but now the tube (the mouthpiece) is so short that the buzzing frequency is almost always below the fundamental pitch; in this region, it is possible to play any pitch, not just those of the harmonic series.

This difference is key to the benefit offered by mouthpiece playing: without the help of the instrument's long tube, locking the buzzing frequency into that of the closest harmonic (or "partial"), the player needs a much more assured sense of pitch to play the desired note. Mouthpiece playing is thus an excellent way to establish the connection between singing in the brain and vibration of the lips, and most often one finds a clearly improved sound quality and ease of playing when the mouthpiece is re-attached to the instrument after this practice.

I recommend playing any music on the mouthpiece, as long as you stay below the fundamental frequency of the mouthpiece—for the trumpet, this is approximately high C (concert B-flat). Above this frequency, the mouthpiece will start to restrict the notes that can be played, by imposing partials. As you play on the mouthpiece, check your pitch accuracy frequently with a piano or other pitch source. Make every effort to play on the mouthpiece with good expression and perfect intonation, as this will strengthen the brain's musical communication to the lips. Be sure to apply all dynamics; because mouthpiece playing is much softer than playing the instrument, there can be a tendency to play everything louder, simply because the general sound level is lower.

Another great benefit of mouthpiece playing is the ability to establish new conditioned reflexes or learned habits. Years of practicing an instrument causes habits to form in the brain, and just holding the instrument can trigger these habits—another illustration of the principle that "neurons that fire together, wire together". Mouthpiece playing offers the possibility of developing helpful new habits, without fighting the old ones, as the instrument is not there to trigger the previously learned behavior. When the brain does not engage the established habits, the strong neural connections, it is free to make new connections. For example, learned habits involving thinking in a mechanical way can be bypassed, in favor of the singing approach. The same goes with muscular patterns involved in breathing and blowing. Practicing the mouthpiece is a bit strange to many players, and this strangeness allows change to happen. We will develop this idea further in the chapter about practicing.

### *Intonation*

We have seen that the ability to hear pitches in one's head is essential for playing a brass instrument, because playing the desired note requires the lips to vibrate at a frequency that can excite the relevant partial in the instrument's air column. Beyond this, however, an even more refined sense of pitch is required, in order to play each note in tune. The task of developing good intonation skills is complicated by the fact that "correct" intonation depends on what other instruments are in the ensemble. Fixed-pitched instruments, such as keyboard instruments, harp and tuned percussion, are typically tuned using a system of equal temperament, in which each octave is divided into 12 equal half-tone intervals. By contrast, string and wind instruments, and unaccompanied voices, are not tied to a fixed set of pitches, so they are able to use just, or "pure", intonation. This tuning system sounds more pleasing to the human ear, as it is based on the natural harmonic series. Equal temperament is a compromise, which allows fixed-pitch instruments to play equally well in tune in every key.

The difference between the two systems can be illustrated as follows. If we start with a fundamental pitch of A2, the note that is two octaves below the standard orchestral tuning note, this has a frequency of 110 cycles per second, or 110 Hz. (For simplicity, we adopt the tuning standard in use in the US and UK.) In the harmonic series, the $2^{nd}$ partial, an octave above the fundamental, has a frequency of 2x110 = 220 Hz; this is the note A3. Similarly, we get the $3^{rd}$ partial (E4) by multiplying the fundamental frequency by 3, yielding 330 Hz, the $4^{th}$ partial (A4) by multiplying by 4 (440 Hz), and so on. In this way, we arrive at the 5th partial (C#5) at 550 Hz, the $6^{th}$ partial (E5) at 660 Hz (E5), the $7^{th}$ partial (G5) at 770 Hz and the $8^{th}$ partial (A5) at 880 Hz. You can see that, continuing upwards, the partials get closer together, soon providing the notes of a diatonic, and then, a chromatic scale.

Already, though, we have enough notes to demonstrate the difference between the two tuning systems. For example, in its just relation to A, the note C#5 has a frequency of 550 Hz, but in equal temperament its frequency is 554.4 Hz—more than 13 percent of a half-tone sharp, compared with its "pure" frequency. More generally, a pure major third comprises two notes with a frequency ratio of 5:4 (1.25), whereas in equal temperament, this ratio is 1.26—a wider interval. By contrast, for a minor third, the pure interval is wider than its equal-temperament counterpart: a frequency ratio of 6:5 (1.2), compared with 1.19. These may seem like small differences, but a brass player who is used to tuning to other brass instruments by listening for nice, resonant chords will find himself having to compensate to stay in tune with a fixed-pitched instrument such as the piano. Similarly, a player who is accustomed to playing with piano will sound out of tune if she plays major or minor thirds using equal temperament in a good brass ensemble. Incidentally, the harmonic series that underlies just intonation also explains why it is so much easier to play in tune in an ensemble whose lower voices, such as trombones and tubas, play with a big, rich sound. Their sound is rich because it contains many overtones—higher harmonics that are easy for the upper voices to hear and tune to. When the lower voices are playing with a deficient sound, poor in overtones, tuning is much more difficult.

### *Playing with others*

The example above, of listening for nice, resonant chords, is just one example of how having good players around you can improve your intonation. A good pianist with a well tuned piano can also help a lot in this regard. If practical or financial considerations preclude frequent sessions with a pianist, a good alternative is the music-learning software SmartMusic, which is relatively inexpensive and easily available on the Web[10]. SmartMusic offers accompaniments for the most common pieces in the wind-instrument repertoire, played by a good imitation of a grand piano. There are also thousands of exercises, scales and arpeggios that can be played with accompaniment in any key or tempo, and with a choice of tuning standard. The software also has an in-built recording device and a metronome. Of course, there is no substitute for a real

---

[10] http://www.smartmusic.com/

pianist, but using a program like SmartMusic is a great way to prepare repertoire before rehearsing with a pianist. By the time you meet the pianist, you will already be familiar with the piano part, and be used to playing in tune with the piano. You can also choose to play the piece on your mouthpiece along with the accompaniment, in your choice of tempo and key.

### *Playing with a drone*

A marvelous way of training your ability to play with just intonation is to play with a drone. This does not refer to an unmanned aircraft, but to a continuous, low tone underlying one's playing. You can obtain a drone by programming an electronic tuner to sound the root of the particular scale, exercise or piece of music that you are practicing.[11] You can start by playing in unison with the drone, and experience the pureness of good intonation, where you hear and feel no "beats", the clashing of vibrations that are not in phase. Then you can do the same with an octave, a fifth and then a major third above the drone. You will soon get used to hearing the major third lower than it would be on a piano tuned to equal temperament, because this lower pitch is where the interval sounds pure, with no beats. Then you can try the sixth—which is just a reversed minor third—then the fourth, the second and the seventh. Now you can play a major scale, and then afterwards try a minor scale. Pretty soon, you will find it possible to fine-tune all the notes of a chromatic scale. You can add a drone to all kinds of scales and exercises, to help you tune the different intervals. This can be especially helpful when playing warm-ups, flexibility exercises and other technical drills, as it forces us to engage the ear (really, the brain's auditory cortex) in the process.

An even greater effect of practicing with a drone for intonation purposes has to do with the development of healthy and efficient sound production. When playing along with a pitch source like the drone, a player will notice that there seems to be a sweet spot where the intonation is 100% pure,

---

11   If you want a richer tone to practice with, you can record your own sound on all the notes of the chromatic scale, and play these samples back as drones. Alternatively, the TonalEnergy tuner app has samples of several instruments, as well as other useful features. For example, it lets you choose between equal temperament and just intonation.

and the instrument resonates optimally. Unfortunately, many players develop the habit of playing with their tuning slide pulled too far out, so that they have to "lip" every note up to be in tune. Doing this means that they will be playing outside the best resonant point of the instrument, so the tone will be deficient in overtones. Moreover, as we will discuss later, the lip muscles have to work quite hard to maintain this high pitch, which will tire them out and lead to endurance and stamina problems. Especially in parts of Europe where the tuning standard is 442–444 Hz, if an American brass instrument (which is usually tuned to 440) has its tuning slide pulled far out, this shows that the player is lipping or forcing the pitch high. When a student sings in his head along with a constant pitch provided by a drone, and puts the tuning slide in a more appropriate position, he can experience playing in the center of each note on the instrument, where it resonates more and therefore sounds better. In this condition, the lips will work less hard, with a greater output, which of course is more efficient for the player.

## Duration

Precise control of the temporal aspects of music making is essential for the musician, for several reasons. First, a defining feature of music is a stable pulse—a constant beat that helps a listener make sense of what he is hearing. A competent player needs to be able to maintain this pulse, and execute rhythms correctly within it. At a more advanced level, the ability to vary pulse and rhythm is an important part of musical expression. And, in ensemble playing, a shared understanding of tempo and rhythm is vital for a piece simply to hold together. At a more mechanistic level, a strong sense of time is what coordinates the widely diverse muscle groups—lips, fingers, tongue and respiratory muscles—that have to function simultaneously when we play a brass instrument. If one were to try to control all of these separate elements individually, the information load on our consciousness would be overwhelming; instead, we can ask for the end product, the desired output, to happen at the correct time, and leave the subconscious brain to "figure out" how to achieve this goal.

A great tool for keeping time and pulse steady is to internally subdivide the rhythm. This secures a shorter distance between beats, so that time will not float. The increased number of beats makes it easier to keep track of time. One's sense of timing can be further developed by listening to and playing with good musicians who possess this skill. And solfège can help with rhythm as well as pitch.

Finally, one can find free or inexpensive apps, or other software, that can help to improve one's sense of time. The most common of these is a metronome, which provides a perfectly stable pulse. Many electronic metronomes also have the ability to subdivide rhythms, so one can learn to be precise at the level of even the smallest rhythmical elements. As mentioned above, SmartMusic has an in-built metronome, or one can use the accompaniment to provide a steady pulse, at any tempo.

Audacity is free recording software that gives visual as well as auditory feedback, and can play back in half-time or slower, so any irregularities will be exposed more clearly. The app SmartRecord works in a similar way. The TonalEnergy tuner, mentioned earlier, has both a drone and a metronome, and can play back recorded files at any tempo. Decades ago, this was done with a dictaphone, a handheld cassette player that could play back the tape at half-tempo. Today, the different tempos are produced digitally, so the half-tempo playback can be either in a lower octave (the only possibility available to the analog dictaphone), or at the original pitch. Finally, the slow-motion mode on the iPhone camera can also play back at slower tempos, with both audio and video.

## Loudness

One of the greatest tools of expression for a brass player is dynamics, as we have at our disposal a dramatic difference between our softest and loudest sounds. It is technically demanding to play at these dynamic extremes, and it is accordingly not unusual for students to play "safe", in a restricted range between mezzopiano and mezzoforte, rather than risk exploring the full dynamic range. As with pitch, rhythm and timbre, control over dynamics is not something innate, but a skill that can be learned and developed, even as an adult.

Before venturing into the extremes, a student should start by exploring the mid-range of dynamics. This is midway between whisper and shout, or between pianississimo (ppp) and fortississimo (fff)—in other words, in the range mezzoforte to forte. Here, we can establish our most beautiful and most easily produced sound, and then try to maintain this sound while we increase the dynamic level to very loud, or decrease it to very soft. Like a good hi-fi system, the character of the sound (for example, the balance between treble and bass) should not change with volume; if we always hear our best sound inside our head, we can learn to produce it throughout our dynamic range.

Here's a possible exercise along these lines. Start by playing a lower-mid-range note (such as middle G, for a trumpet player) at a forte dynamic, with the fattest and most resonant sound you can produce; then apply a diminuendo, keeping the same tone quality. This can be done by studying the way you blow in forte, and then changing the speed of the air—blowing more slowly to play more softly. Be careful not to change the tongue position to form a higher vowel, such as "ee", as this can sharpen the pitch and thin the tone. If your basic vowel for forte mid-range playing is a low vowel such as "oh" or "ah", it is important to maintain this as you change the dynamic level, as the "thick" airstream will help you to keep the same sound quality and intonation. The thick air is a constant, through all dynamics; all that changes is the air speed. Of course, one may sometimes want to play with a different sound, for purposes of musical expression. For example, by consciously choosing an "ee" vowel—which creates a thinner airstream, and hence a thinner sound—one can produce a "veiled pianissimo". Later, we will discuss whether tongue position can be used for facilitating high range, as is often taught, or if changing vowels is mostly appropriate for color changes.

To attain a refined control of dynamics, a student can practice "scales" of dynamics, analogous to conventional scales of pitch. For example, he can go through a wide range of dynamic markings (f to mf to mp to p to pp, or vice versa) on a single note. It may help to associate each dynamic level with a number, which can be thought of as a speedometer reading for the air speed. This will strengthen the mental connection between air speed and dynamic level. Using higher numbers for faster air (louder playing) and lower numbers for slower air (softer playing), a diminuendo from forte could be 5, 4, 3, 2, 1 (corresponding to f, mf, mp, p, pp) and a crescendo from pianissimo 1, 2, 3, 4, 5 (for pp, p, mp, mf, f). The scale can then be expanded to eight numbers, going from fff to ppp and back, and then combined with the eight steps of a diatonic scale—playing with a drone, to keep the intonation consistent. Pretty soon, the student will find that his dynamic sensitivity is developing nicely, and he will have better control of air speed and more responsive lips throughout the entire dynamic range. These abilities—both to hear, and to be able to produce, finer and finer differences in dynamic level—provide the musician with an excellent tool for phrasing, using subtle changes in this dimension.

Different dynamic levels are usually accompanied by different degrees of effort, and it often happens that brass players start to monitor the effort they are expending, instead of the actual acoustical output. For example, players may associate loud playing with strong exertion of the muscles involved in breathing, and soft playing with holding the breath and/or closing the airways. This can lead a player who is exploring the dynamic range to change the quality of her sound along with—or even more than—its volume: loud playing takes on a rough, forced sound, and soft playing becomes a thin tone, deficient in overtones and color. In some cases, a composer may ask for such colors, but in classical music this is the exception, rather than the rule. Using a decibel meter for practicing dynamics can be a big help, as the meter (which can be downloaded as a free smartphone app) measures the actual sound output, rather than how a player is feeling. Positioning the device at a fixed distance from the instrument's bell will help the player to establish a consistent control over dynamic levels from day to day.

## Timbre

Timbre is a French word, adopted into English, which is used to describe tone color or quality. In acoustics, it is best defined as a sound's frequency spectrum—the relative contributions made to a tone by its fundamental pitch and each of its harmonics, or overtones. When two different instruments play the same pitch, at the same loudness, it is the timbre that makes them sound different from each other. With a refined sense of timbre, we are able to distinguish among musicians who play the same instrument, but with different, individually personal, sounds.

As discussed above, the sense of timbre is very much related to that of pitch, as what we perceive as a tone comprises the fundamental pitch and its harmonics. Also, when it comes to creating a beautiful sound on a brass instrument, the ability to buzz the correct pitch into the instrument determines whether a note will have its optimal resonance, and hence its best tone quality.

Later, when discussing embouchure and breathing, we will see that a beautiful sound results from a good cooperation between the lips' vibration and the aerodynamics that are created by the respiratory system—in other words, from a player's technique. Yet players who produce an amazing sound can be unaware of how they do it, as several different body structures are involved, and the control of some of them is beyond conscious awareness. If the player has a sufficiently strong concept of tone, this should be enough to control the relevant muscles, and make the player sound great. The best way to check whether you are playing with a healthy technique is to listen to your sound; a great sound is a sure sign that your physiology is working well. By contrast, you may be conscientious about doing everything "correctly", as regards embouchure, breathing, tongue position, and the like, but if you are not sounding great, you are missing the point.

An efficient way to develop a great sense of tone quality is to listen to great players. A rich tone on a brass instrument cannot be encapsulated in words. Try to develop a huge brain-library of amazing brass sounds, by searching out players playing repertoire across the ages, from Renaissance polyphony to contemporary jazz. Listen to different players play the same music, to compare their sounds. Go to many live concerts, to hear the real sound in a concert hall, and search out great players for lessons, persuading them to demonstrate their playing for you. Finally, extend your library of sounds beyond the brass world, by listening to great musicians on other instruments, especially those with stronger soloistic traditions, such as violinists, pianists and, especially, singers.

The good brass player should be able to play with an even timbre at all pitches and dynamic levels, and with any type of articulation—for aesthetic reasons, certainly, but also because, as discussed above, a beautiful sound indicates healthy basic tone production. Later, when this is accomplished, the student can add different colors for purposes of phrasing and expression; but often players will, for example, sound thin in the high range and be stuck in this color, without the ability to choose whatever suits the musical context.

If the student can copy the open, free sound of the mid-range into the high range, he will establish good habits there. Many warm-up exercises start in the middle register and move progressively higher; when playing these, instead of merely playing the notes, the student should focus explicitly on maintaining the same sound quality in the high register.

The Long Tone Studies by Vincent Cichowicz are excellent for this purpose. They are cantabile in nature, start in the mid-range, and are designed to make the player move gradually throughout the register while maintaining a good sound. Unlike a runner warming up her legs for a 100-meter sprint, a brass player doesn't need to increase the blood supply to her lips when warming up; this is indicated by the fact that her lips are already red. Warming up for a brass player is more about establishing one's concept of sound in easy music, and transferring it into different registers, dynamics and articulations.

Another good exercise in this context is playing octave slurs. Order the best imaginable sound when playing in the mid- to low range, and just before slurring to the higher octave, sing the upper pitch mentally, with the same sound quality as the lower octave. More generally, Arnold Jacobs spoke of letting the great sounds established on easier notes "become the teacher" of the following notes. In other words, sound great on the first note and let this teach the second note; let the second note be the teacher of the third note; and so on.

Often, the highest note of a phrase captures the brass player's attention, so he forgets to take care of the quality of the easier notes preceding it. Allowing these notes to sound mediocre (which, you will recall, indicates a less than optimal technique) will only ensure that the player has a struggling embouchure even before getting to the highest note. It is better to focus on the note *before* the high one, always copying the sound of one good note to the next.

## FOCUSING ON THE SONG

As the brass student improves her facility with the four musical parameters described in the previous chapter, she can begin to rely more and more on "the song in the head" to guide the lip and other structures involved in the physical execution of playing. As the internal song is mental in nature, and thus as fragile as a thought, one's mind needs to be quite focused to sustain it.

One way of maintaining the required focus is to subdivide each musical phrase into smaller groups of notes, or subphrases. In this way, instead of having to comprehend the hundreds or thousands of notes that comprise a piece, one can focus on the smaller and more specific task of executing small groups of notes. This increases the chance that one's mind will stay absorbed in the present and immediate future, rather than wandering off to analyze and judge what has already been played, or worry about what difficulties may lie ahead. When the mind wanders in this way, the player loses the ability to pay proper attention to the notes that she is playing right now—the kind of attention required for the correct neurological message to be sent to the physical structures that are responsible for playing these notes. This inattention can result in missed notes, a mediocre sound or non-expressive playing. Arnold Jacobs would use phrases such as: "don't screw up the easy notes just because you have a hard one coming up"; "instead of *playing* the phrase, *create* the phrase note by note as you go"; "audiences hear phrases, and performers build phrases note by note"; or "try to have subphrases within the large phrase. Mentally you are more efficient in the brain with small groups of numbers."

This last phenomenon referred to by Jacobs is well known in psychology as "chunking"[12] [13]: it is much easier to remember a sequence of numbers when they are arranged in groups. For example, the phone number 987563978 is much easier to remember when written as 987-563-978. Similarly, the sentence, "thissentencemakessensebecauseallthelettersaregroupedintowords" is easier to decode when chunked into "this sentence makes sense because all the letters are grouped into words"—even though, when we hear the words being spoken, there is no audible space between them.

Chunking may also help with musical expression. In his book, *Note Grouping: A Method for Achieving Expression and Style in Musical Performance*, James Morgan Thurmond explores the possibilities of adding expression to phrasing by grouping notes together as being "upbeatish" towards a downbeat. Thurmond adopts terminology from Greek poetry, in which a weak syllable or word is referred to as "arsis" (literally, "the raising of the foot in beating time", or upbeat), and a strong syllable or word is "thesis" (the lowering of the foot, or downbeat). According to Thurmond, being aware of each note's role as either arsis or thesis will give more life and expression to the music being played. The smallest form of musical motif has only two notes, with the first one usually being an arsis and the second one a thesis. The role of the arsis is to lead towards the thesis, and the role of the thesis is to be the result of this—very much like tension followed by relaxation. Constantly grouping notes together in these small units can facilitate the forward movement of the phrase, and help the brass player to maintain focus on the mental singing of each note as he advances through the passage in question.

---

[12] Neath, Ian & Surprenant, Aimée M. *Human Memory: An Introduction to Research, Data, and Theory* (Wadsworth Cengage Learning, 2003), pp. 47-48: "Chunking in psychology is a process by which individual pieces of information are bound together into a meaningful whole."

[13] Tulving, Endel & Craik, Fergus I. M. *The Oxford Handbook of Memory* (Oxford University Press, 2000), p. 12: "A chunk is defined as a familiar collection of more elementary units that have been inter-associated and stored in memory repeatedly and act as a coherent, integrated group when retrieved."

This is very unlike the way music is generally notated, with notes either separated or, in the case of shorter notes such as eighths or sixteenths, grouped for the sake of reading, rather than as an indication of how they should be executed musically.[14] For instance, in a bar with four groups of four sixteenth notes, they are traditionally notated as if they all belong to the beat just reached (Fig. 1), whereas a more fluent way of grouping the notes would be going *towards* the next beat (Fig. 2). Figure 3 shows the same principle applied to an excerpt from the trumpet repertoire.

**Figure 1.** Traditional notation, with notes grouped to facilitate reading.

**Figure 2.** The same sixteenth notes as in Fig. 1, showing how they can be performed if their thesis and arsis roles (T and A) are taken into consideration. Grouping the notes in this way gives more direction towards the main beats than if the notation in Fig. 1 is followed literally.

---

14   McGill, David. *Sound in Motion: A Performer's Guide to Greater Musical Expression* (Indiana University Press, 2009).

**Figure 3.** An example of subphrases applied to Arthur Honegger's Intrada. The last note in each group is a thesis, with the preceding notes leading to it, ensuring directional playing consistent with the arsis-thesis relationship. Each subphrase is a building block in the larger phrases, which have their own demands of intensifying towards and relaxing away from climaxes, sustaining longer lines, and so forth. Of course, faster passages can be grouped into larger chunks.

This note grouping gives a much more directional way of playing, in which the energy from an upbeat driving to its resulting downbeat keeps the music flowing, and simultaneously guarantees the performer's involvement and focus in the moment as she proceeds, executing only a few notes at a time. This approach can also make the performer more aware of the music's harmonic structure, in which, for example, a dominant chord drives towards its resultant tonic. Often, wind players will breathe on bar lines, which can sever the connection between a dominant and a tonic, or more generally between an upbeat and its resultant downbeat.

Although at any moment a player will be focusing his attention on playing the small subphrases, he must still, of course, have an overall plan for the larger phrases—including building up to climaxes with dynamics, intensity of vibrato, and so forth—and, indeed, for the piece as a whole.

## THE EMBOUCHURE

The brass player's embouchure is a complex phenomenon, in which intricate movements of facial muscles have to coordinate precisely with aerodynamic functions of the breathing apparatus, all in a way that works with the acoustical laws governing the instrument. When a brass player buzzes her lips inside the mouthpiece, air is passing between the lips and making them vibrate. This cooperation between the lips and the airstream is so strong that acousticians define the brass player's embouchure as an "aerodynamic unit", along with the human voice. The lips cannot vibrate or buzz without the airstream exciting them, and the air cannot make anything but a hissing sound in the instrument without the lips' vibration.

When a brass player plays very softly, he may have the feeling that his lips are vibrating without any air moving through them, but this is just an illusion; there is no nerve in the lips that can make them vibrate with the frequency necessary for playing tones on a brass instrument without an airstream. Similarly, a brass player may sometimes feel that her lips are not vibrating at all when playing, but if this were true there would be no tone, only a hissing sound. Once the air has made the lips vibrate, it has no purpose for playing, and could be let out the side if necessary; the air blown into the trumpet is a waste product. We don't blow the trumpet; we blow the lips, and the lips buzz the trumpet—or, more precisely, the air column inside the trumpet.

When a brass player plays a note, his lips vibrate at a frequency that depends on the desired pitch. The familiar buzzing sound is made by the lips opening and closing at a rate of anything from hundreds to several thousands of times per second.[15] Positive air pressure inside the mouth ("blowing") causes the lips to send a pressure wave through the tube of the brass instrument. When the wave reaches the bell it is reflected back to the lips, arriving there at exactly the right time for another wave to be sent—at least, this will be the case if the lips are buzzing a pitch that can

---

15   It can be less than a hundred times per second when playing low notes on low brass instruments, and more than a thousand times per second when playing into the extreme high range on the trumpet.

resonate in the instrument's air column, as determined by its length.[16] The travelling back and forth creates a standing wave inside the tube, with a frequency corresponding to one of the tones of the harmonic series. A fraction of the energy in the standing wave will leak out of the tube, into the surrounding room (creating the instrument's sound), but most of the oscillations will be reflected, maintaining the standing wave.[17]

The brass player needs to be able to constantly change the lips' vibration frequency, according to the demands of the music. Even embouchures that look "stable" from the outside, showing very little movement, have significant movement happening inside the rim of the mouthpiece—as can be seen by deploying a video camera inside the mouthpiece.[18] In such videos, a trained trumpet embouchure is seen to have an oval-shaped opening (often called the aperture), with the lips vibrating at its edges. It thus resembles a set of oboe reeds of different sizes, forming smaller apertures when ascending in pitch, and larger ones when descending.

Beyond pitch and its corresponding vibration frequency, the versatile brass player can change other properties of the embouchure, to provide variations in dynamics and timbre. Because the brass player's embouchure is constantly changing to provide the desired output, it is counterproductive to try to follow "rules" about the embouchure, that dictate a specific way of holding the lips to function properly. Such rules are likely to limit the freedom of movement that is so important for the lips to be able to deliver the optimal output. The only constant about an embouchure is that it is a variable.

The physics of vibrating materials tells us that the vibration frequency of the lips will be determined primarily by their mass, stiffness and tension. When changing pitch, the brass player will accordingly need to change

---

16    One can imagine how quickly the pressure waves are moving, by thinking of sixteenth notes played at a metronome marking of 120. At this tempo, one quarter note lasts half a second, so a sixteenth note must last 0.125 seconds. Even in such a short time, a player's lips playing an A4 (440 Hz) will oscillate 440 x 0.125 = 55 times.
17    Steenstrup, Kristian: *Teaching Brass, 2nd revised edition* (Royal Academy of Music, Aarhus, 2007).
18    http://www.lipcam.de/

one or more of these factors. Starting with mass, the less mass that is vibrating, the higher the pitch. But the vibrating lip mass is not easy to change while playing, as this is determined by the mouthpiece rim's slight compression, which isolates the part that will vibrate; the portion of the lips inside the rim is the mass that we work with. One can reduce this mass by choosing a rim with a smaller diameter, and this will make it easier to play higher pitches; but there will be limitations in the mid- to low range, especially in sound quality. This is why lead players typically use a smaller rim than do symphonic players, and why most classical players change to a smaller rim when playing piccolo trumpet.

For any rim size, a puckered embouchure (as when saying WOH) will provide more lip mass inside the rim, available for vibration, than a stretched embouchure. As we will see, a puckered embouchure has the potential to increase its vibration frequency by increasing its stiffness and/or tension inside the rim. In contrast, a stretched embouchure, which starts out with a higher characteristic vibration frequency because of the smaller mass and starting tension, may not have the capacity to access lower pitches, without somehow adding mass to the vibrating lips. Some players address this problem by changing their setting, using stretched, thin lips for the high range and thicker lips for the low range. But it is obvious that doing this would limit one's ability to negotiate register changes and large intervals without having to make a break to reset the embouchure.

Stiffness and tension act in the opposite direction to mass: as they increase, so does the vibration frequency. Although we don't know exactly what happens inside the mouthpiece while we are playing, and even the greatest players may not be aware of exactly what they are doing, we can infer that, to go to a higher note, a player must contrive to increase the stiffness and/or tension of the lips. Stiffness might be increased by contracting the lips towards the center, or by compressing them against each other vertically; tension can be added (possibly along with stiffness) by stretching the lips in a smile. If the embouchure corners are held firm, it may be possible to add tension without smiling. Applying more mouthpiece pressure may also add tension or stiffness, as well as thinning the lips, decreasing their mass. We know, however, that the price for excessive mouthpiece pressure, as well as for stretched lips (as in smiling), can be bruising under the rim and/or loss of blood circulation to the center of the lips. Beyond this capacity for damage, stretched or thinned lips will produce a "thinner" sound, with a smaller contribution from lower harmonics.

To maintain a big, "orchestral" sound, rich in the lower harmonics, one should keep the lip mass relatively large (a relaxed and puckered embouchure) and supplied with a large airflow. This will most often produce a richer and rounder sound than a stretched and thinned embouchure. Ascending into the high range will require changes to the embouchure, but the player must ensure, by monitoring her sound, that the lips do not get too stiff, tense, stretched or traumatized by excessive mouthpiece force.

With several variables affecting the lips' vibration frequency, the brass player has a range of ways, consciously or unconsciously, to produce any desired pitch. But this can cause problems in the real world. For example, if the lip muscles are not strong enough to sustain a given pitch, the brain may step in to "help" by stretching the lips in a smile and/or pressing the mouthpiece harder against the lips. As already mentioned, this can damage the function of the lips, causing problems with endurance and stamina.

In the high register, when the lips are more rigid and the aperture is smaller, a stronger aerodynamic force is required to get the lips to vibrate; this explains why brass players often find themselves supplying increasingly high air pressure as they ascend in pitch. If the respiratory system is unable to supply enough energy to excite the lips, they will cease to vibrate—the note will stop. As we will discuss later, there can be many reasons why the lungs fail to supply the right aerodynamic force. A downward-contracted diaphragm could be acting as an antagonistic muscle, canceling out the work of the expiratory muscles; the airway could be blocked by the tongue, or by closures in the throat, or there could be an insufficient volume of air in the lungs to generate the required power. Most often, failures or inefficiencies in the breathing apparatus are felt in the lips, even though the cause is elsewhere.

Frequently, we may experience the opposite problem—namely, that the aerodynamic power provided is excessive for a given pitch and dynamic level. For example, we may hear a brass player playing in the middle register, yet applying a degree of effort appropriate to playing an octave higher. This practice, referred to as "overblowing," or "forcing", results in a less than ideal sound quality. In addition, the application of excessive aerodynamic force implies that the lips are not resonating efficiently, meaning that the musculature is having to work harder than necessary. This can cause exhaustion, leading to the need to compensate, with unfortunate consequences as discussed above.

We can see that the potential combinations of the different factors pertaining to embouchure are abundant. Moreover, the properties of the embouchure need to change quickly, to keep pace with the changing pitches, dynamics and sound quality of the music. Rather than try to control these complex combinations consciously while playing, the brass player will find it more fruitful to order the musical product—namely, correct, in-tune pitch and full sound, accompanied by plentiful air supply at the lips. If the player is making a great sound, then, by definition, the properties of the embouchure must be correct. Controlling one's embouchure is not done by consciously manipulating muscles, but by mentally singing, which will send instructions to the lips in the same unconscious way as a singer communicates her intentions to the vocal cords.

These insights lead to two paramount motivations for the brass player, which are mutually supporting:

1. Sound greater.
2. Make it easier.

As we have seen, when we sound great it is because our muscles are working efficiently; and when we play easily, with the use of minimal effort, most often the resultant sound will be richer.

## Free buzzing

Some brass-playing methods recommend "free buzzing"— buzzing the lips alone, without the mouthpiece or instrument—as a way to encourage efficient vibration of the lips. Indeed, with careful monitoring of pitch, and of the quality of the vibration, free buzzing can establish a good connection between singing in the brain and the response of the lip tissue; but it can also cause problems. In normal playing, the mouthpiece rim compresses the lips gently, thereby isolating the lip outside the rim from the vibrating mass inside. In the absence of a mouthpiece rim, the facial muscles have to do this job of isolating the vibrating part of the embouchure, and are accordingly called on to exert more effort than is normally required. In particular, the large, powerful muscles of the cheeks will start to overpower the smaller, more delicate muscles in the center of the lip. The embouchure may then become very muscular and resistant, and soon the breath will have to work harder to force the lips to vibrate.

## The rim

The problem just mentioned can be avoided by buzzing with a mouthpiece rim, in the form of a screw rim, a cut-off mouthpiece, or a visualizer on a stick. Even here, the student has to be cautious, as there is no standing wave helping the lips to vibrate. To avoid over-working the lips, one should play for only about a minute (or at most, a minute and a half) at a time, only in the low to middle register, and not very loudly. Such short periods of working with the rim can be repeated many times during the day, without doing any harm.

It is important to think of buzzing on the rim as a way to sense one's vibrating lips, and improve the quality of the vibration, rather than building strength or developing muscles. For this reason, playing brief melodies with musical expression will be more beneficial than playing technical exercises. Practicing passages of music an octave below their normal pitch is a good way to increase responsiveness, and move away from a resistant, non-vibrant lip. Alternating between playing on the rim and on the instrument can also be a helpful tactic. We cannot feel the vibration when playing the instrument, but, having just felt it when playing on the rim, we can pretend to feel it afterwards on the horn, so that we are not judging vibration at the rim, but inside it, at the vibrating surface.

Buzzing on the rim can also help a player solve problems with articulation. If the tongue blocks the airstream unnecessarily, this can interfere with sound quality and ease of playing. Practicing tongued passages on the rim keeps the player's focus on the continuous vibration of the lips, rather than the interruptions to the air.

### Sensing the vibrating surface

The brass player makes contact with the instrument where his hands hold it, and where the mouthpiece presses on his lips, but none of these contact points is where the sound is generated. The tone is produced where the lips vibrate, *inside* the mouthpiece rim, but this vibrating tissue is difficult to feel. Instead, we feel the mouthpiece pressure against the lips—perhaps especially so when playing in the high register. Before practicing a high passage, a student can gently scratch the surface of the lips in the center, where vibration must occur, with a fingernail or the edge of a mouthpiece. Afterwards, when playing, the brain will examine the irritated area and start to engage the vibration there, rather than attempting it at the rim. There should be emphasis on the vibration, not the resistance to it, to maximize the responsiveness of the lips.

### Contact pressure

Often, a player will miss the first note of an entry, even when it is no more difficult than the notes that follow. This may result from not having heard the correct pitch in advance; but another possibility is that the player had insufficient contact pressure at the beginning of the note. The vibrating portion of the lip must be separated from the rest of the lip before the first note is played, so that the fine muscles that shape the center of the lips can do their work. This problem will most often occur when a student has been trying to learn to play using no mouthpiece pressure, or extremely little.

### High range

Playing in the high range can be challenging for the brass player. This is especially true for trumpet players, for whom the repertoire of the Baroque and modern periods can be particularly testing. As discussed above, the embouchure is quite complex, with many factors influencing each other, and it can be difficult to attain facility in the high register by consciously manipulating muscles, or by theory. Also, even with the most efficient and relaxed approach, more effort is needed to maintain the lip contraction required to play in this register (to make smaller and smaller oboe reeds), so the small muscles that shape the vibrating surface—the retractors, protractors, elevators and depressors—have to be built up over time.

For these reasons, the only way to develop a good high range is to play there. As the student is working at the limit of her abilities, she must accept imperfection at first, and from this, develop skill. The student must be encouraged not to avoid this range, just because it feels and sounds less than ideal. As Arnold Jacobs used to say, "Bad notes can be made into good notes; silence can't" and, "you don't start with skill; you start with crudity, and from crudity you develop skill." First "get" the note, and then immediately begin to establish beauty of tone, as a good sound reflects an efficient technique. The following guidelines can be recommended for working in the high range:

At most, 20% of the daily practice time should be spent playing at any extreme—but especially at the high end of one's range.

1. Rest frequently.
2. Play very lyrically, as this stimulates beauty of sound.
3. Play nice ballads or lyrical tunes in the high range, rather than exercises, to stimulate the singing approach.
4. Develop your lip muscles at moderate dynamic levels (mp to mf), so the lips are not being forced into vibrating by a powerful airstream.
5. Establish your ability to play high notes in legato at first, to avoid the complications of the tongue blocking the supply of air to the lips. Add tonguing later, when good production and sound have been established.
6. Use vibrato to let the lips find where each note resonates best. The point of best resonance is not always where the intonation is correct, as on any instrument the higher notes tend to be less well in tune. This vibrato is for therapeutic reasons: it allows the lips to resonate with the instrument's air column, at least part of the time, while disguising the intonation problems by averaging over the varying

pitch. This therapeutic vibrato can be turned off, as appropriate for the musical and stylistic context. A tasteful vibrato can of course also be used as an expressive tool, but the therapeutic vibrato is specifically meant to help with tone production.

7. The higher you play, the less resonance the instrument's air column provides, to help the lips vibrate; this is partly why it is harder to produce a stable tone there, and why stamina is a problem in the high range. You can get the same effect by playing the mouthpiece alone, as here again there is no standing wave to help the lips vibrate. Practicing the mouthpiece, even an octave lower than the pitches you are aiming for, will benefit your high range.

8. Practice playing a higher-pitched instrument: piccolo trumpet for the trumpet player, alto trombone for the trombonist, and baritone horn or euphonium for the tubist. The pitches that are located in the high register of the bigger horns are in the mid- to low range of these instruments, making them better resonators. This makes it easier for the lips to vibrate at these pitches, and to build up the tissue for playing them. The facility established on the smaller horn can be transferred to the bigger one, leading to a more rapid improvement of the high range.

9. Make sure you breathe fully and frequently when working in the high range. Although the volume of air required to play in the high range is less than for lower notes, the air pressure needed to vibrate the lips is higher, so the lungs (really, the expiratory muscles) need to compress more to generate this. The fuller the lungs, the easier it is to compress the air.

## BREATHING

Scientific descriptions of the aerodynamics of brass playing usually use the terms air pressure and airflow. Air pressure is the force (per unit area) acting on the lips, whereas airflow refers to the volume of air (per unit time) passing through the lips. Brass players usually feel that they blow with higher air pressure when they play higher notes. While this is confirmed by tests,[19] it is not the case that ascending into a higher register is accomplished by an increase in air pressure alone. As discussed in the previous chapter, ascending in pitch requires appropriate changes in the stiffness and/or tension of the lips, which in turn demand an increase in air pressure, to secure the vibration. If increased air pressure is applied to an unchanged embouchure, the result will be a louder sound, rather than a higher pitch. Logically, one can conclude that playing both higher and louder will demand a significant increase in air pressure.

Airflow has the opposite relation to pitch. Descending in range requires a more relaxed (less tense or stiff) embouchure, allowing more air to pass through the lips—in other words, an increased airflow. Tests have confirmed that airflow increases and air pressure decreases when descending in pitch[20], and that this inverse relationship between flow and pressure applies across the pitch range, at constant dynamic level.

As discussed earlier, a rich, round sound comes from playing with more relaxed lips and greater airflow. We can now see that the greater airflow results naturally from the relaxation of the lips. This effect can be further enhanced by playing with a shorter horn (tuning slide further in), so that the player will relax down into the center of the tone—as described in the section on working with a drone. Thus, a round, "fat" sound, rich in lower harmonics, and accompanied by more relaxed lips, larger airflow and lower intonation, stands in opposition to a thin sound, poor in lower harmonics, accompanied by tight lips, restricted airflow and higher

---

19    Kruger, Jonathan et al. More air, less air, what is air? *ITG Journal* March 2012, 12-19.
20    Kruger, Jonathan et al. A comparative study of air support in the trumpet, horn, trombone and tuba. In Baroni, M. et al. *Proceedings of the 9th International Conference on Music Perception and Cognition*, University of Bologna (2006).

intonation. Arnold Jacobs encapsulated this distinction, and encouraged students to focus on airflow, by talking about "thick air" versus "thin air"—although he also emphasized the role of the embouchure (relaxed versus tight) in effecting this change. One can easily feel, when blowing on the back of a hand, how a tight, constricted embouchure blows a thinner airstream, whereas a more relaxed embouchure, accompanied by a low tongue position, blows a thicker column of air.

In what follows we will discuss some of the factors pertaining to breathing and its role in brass playing. In particular, we will distinguish between two different descriptions of the breathing process: the physiology of breathing, which is based on a mechanistic, physical view of the operation of the lungs and associated muscles; and the psychology of breathing, which describes how we perceive air in brass playing—and, not least, how we control it.

## Physiology of breathing

The basics physics of breathing is simple, prompting one to wonder why its description is often complicated, and occasionally mystified throughout the world. Just as water flows downhill, or heat is transferred from a hotter to a colder object, air molecules tend to flow from an area with higher air pressure to one with lower pressure. The result is wind, or air movement.

This is what happens when we breathe. Our inspiratory muscles expand the lungs, increasing their volume. At the instant of expansion, the same number of air molecules find themselves occupying a larger volume, meaning that the air pressure inside the lungs will be lower than the atmospheric pressure outside the body. Immediately (unless the nose and mouth are closed), air from outside will flow into the lungs to attempt to equalize this pressure difference. When the lungs are full, or when the inspiratory muscles stop contracting, the elasticity of the lungs and/or contraction of the expiratory muscles will collapse and then compress the lungs. As the volume decreases, the air pressure inside increases to above atmospheric pressure, causing the air to flow out of the lungs.

This pressure–volume relationship is expressed in a law of physics, Boyle's Law, which states that, all else being equal, the pressure of a gas is inversely proportional to the volume it occupies. So, when we increase the volume of the lungs, the pressure inside goes down, and when we decrease the volume of the lungs, the pressure goes up. This is the simple mechanics of getting air in and out of the lungs. It is very much like a bellows system, where enlarging the bellows causes air to be sucked in, and compressing them blows air out. This is a universal law of physics, which must be obeyed regardless of what method of breathing you are taught, or what you believe in.

The muscles that expand and compress the lungs are those surrounding the chest. The main inspiratory muscle is the diaphragm, which contracts downwards, making the lungs longer and expanding the lower chest. When the diaphragm moves down, it displaces the organs of the abdomen, making it look as if we are "breathing with the belly", but the diaphragm and lungs do not extend so low. The diaphragm, like all muscles, can only contract or relax—the latter term referring to a passive absence of contraction. The diaphragm contracts downward and relaxes upwards, so it is active only when we are breathing in, and passive when we are blowing out. Despite this, students are still taught to "blow from the diaphragm", even though this is physiologically impossible: the diaphragm can only lower the air pressure in the lungs, not raise it. Other inspiratory muscles include the external intercostals, which raise the ribs, thereby expanding the lungs upwards. There are also other, less important inspiratory muscles, known as the accessory muscles, but these are not important for normal breathing in wind playing.

Note that breathing occurs mostly in the front, where—if the player's posture is properly tall and relaxed—the chest will rise and the abdomen will fall as the lungs expand. Contrary to the beliefs of some pedagogical circles, the back is not capable of breathing. The back is mostly engaged in posture, and shows very little movement itself, as the ribs are quite close to each other here, so they rotate, but do not allow for much expansion.[21]

When blowing out, according to Boyle's Law, the lungs need to get

---

21   A more detailed explanation can be found in Steenstrup, Kristian. *Teaching Brass, 2nd revised edition* (Royal Academy of Music, Aarhus, 2007).

smaller. Their elasticity (and that of the surrounding cartilage) causes them to collapse when we stop using the inspiratory muscles; this creates quite a bit of outward airflow, even though we are just relaxing. This is what we experience when letting the air out with a sigh after a big breath, and the energy in this air is sometimes called the "positive relaxation pressure". When we need to blow with more power than this—for example, for high and loud trumpet playing—or when we need to blow a large volume of air, as for loud, low playing on the tuba, our expiratory muscles assist the elasticity of the lungs and the collapse of the chest by compressing the lungs further. The muscles responsible for this compression are the abdominal muscles, in the lower part of the torso,[22] and the internal intercostals, which compress the chest. When the diaphragm relaxes and ascends, it allows the abdominal muscles to move inward, pushing air out of the lungs in the lower torso.

We have seen that the inspiratory muscles expand the lungs, sucking air in; and the expiratory muscles and elastic recoil of the lungs and rib cage compress the lungs, blowing air out. When a brass player breathes naturally, his chest and abdominal region are in constant motion. When the player inhales, the chest rises and the abdomen moves down and out; when the player exhales and plays the instrument, the abdomen moves in and the chest falls. If the diaphragm is relaxed, allowing the abdominal muscles to contract inward, these muscles will normally not have to work very hard. Playing high and/or loudly will require more work from the abdominal muscles, but still less than if they have to work against a downward-contracted diaphragm. When a brass player is using a lot of air, to play loudly or in the extreme low register, the chest and abdominal movements will be faster than when air use is minimal. But whenever a sound is being produced, air has to move, so there will always be some movement in these parts of the body, rather than the static clenching of antagonistic muscles working isometrically against each other, with no consequent movement of air.

Between the diaphragm and the abdominal muscles we have the visceral

---

22  These are powerful muscles in four layers: the rectus abdominis, transversus abdominis, and the interior and exterior oblique muscles.

organs, including the liver, bladder, stomach and intestines. Simultaneous contraction of the diaphragm and the abdominal muscles will squeeze the intestines, rather than the lungs; indeed, one of the secondary jobs of these respiratory muscles is to expel feces from the bowel. Another job is the protection of the visceral organs in combat, by hardening the abdominal wall against the downward-contracted diaphragm. Both of these functions can also trigger closure of the throat. These are natural functions, installed as reflexes very early in human evolution—and certainly well before the invention of wind instruments. Accordingly, these functions are very easily triggered—especially when fear is involved, as can happen when experiencing performance anxiety. These functions can also be unhelpfully learned as conditioned reflexes, associated with the playing of the instrument, for example, as part of the so called "tight-gut method", which advocates isometric contraction as a mistaken attempt to apply breath power or "support" for playing. Unfortunately, this method is still being taught in some institutions, but fortunately less and less as better science is applied.

Lungs that are nearly full have a higher potential expiratory power, because of the positive relaxation pressure: the emptier the lungs, the more it is necessary to contract expiratory musculature to squeeze air out of them. A player can thus expel quite a bit of air from full lungs, simply by relaxing the inspiratory muscles; by contrast, lungs that are nearly empty expel relatively little air, even when the expiratory muscles work hard. Moreover, when the lungs get close to empty, the subconscious brain stimulates the diaphragm to initiate inhalation, so the abdominal muscles, which are contracting to continue blowing out, now have to fight against this opposing contraction. For these reasons, it is better to play on relatively full lungs. As the positive relaxation pressure reaches zero at around 40% of the vital capacity, one should try to play in the upper two-thirds of one's lung capacity, going below this point only in emergency situations, when there is no opportunity to take another breath.

## Posture

There are some physiological reasons why good posture is important for breathing. When a wind player stands as tall as possible, but without overstretching any muscles, the thorax can move more freely than is the case for a player with poor posture. When posture is good, the rib cage is free to move up, and doesn't hinder the descent of the diaphragm by compressing the abdominal region. In this standing position, the spinal column naturally assumes an arch in the lumbar–dorsal region, from which the ribs can rotate easily, accommodating full thoracic breathing.[23] Often, when brass players sit down, they collapse—perhaps to feel more relaxed— and will frequently notice impaired playing, when compared with the erect standing position. By thinking of sitting tall from the hips up, and by keeping a similar curve in the lumbar region as when standing, a player can attempt to maintain the same conditions for the rib cage, although it may be difficult to attain the same efficiency of breathing.[24]

Several popular body therapies advocate contraction of the abdominal muscles to support the postural activity of the back muscles, but for the wind player this would impair the flexibility of the abdominal region, necessary for the alternation between contraction of the diaphragm for breathing in, and of the abdominal muscles for breathing out.

Another reason for maintaining good posture is acoustical, particularly for trumpet and trombone players. Because the lower harmonics spread in all directions, whereas the higher harmonics are very directional, the orientation of the instrument will affect how the audience hears the sound. Poor posture, causing the bell of the instrument to point downwards, rather than into the concert hall, will remove higher overtones (and hence brilliance) from the sound.

A final reason for good posture is neurochemical, and relates to how our posture affects our mindset and attitude—important factors in determining our response to high-pressure situations, and combating performance anxiety. A study[25] of 42 volunteers, performed by researchers from Harvard and Columbia universities, had the subjects

---

23    Lin, F. et al. Effect of different sitting postures on lung capacity, expiratory flow, and lumbar lordosis. *Archives of Physical Medicine and Rehabilitation* 87, 504-509 (2006).
24    Price, K. et al. The effect of standing and sitting postures on breathing in brass players. *Springerplus* 3: **210** (2014). doi: 10.1186/2193-1801-3-210.
25    Carney, D.R. et al. Power posing: brief nonverbal displays affect neuroendocrine levels and risk tolerance. *Psychological Science* 21, 1363-1368 (2010).

hold two "high-power" or two "low-power" poses, for one minute each. The high-power poses were expansive positions, with open limbs, whereas the low-power poses were contractive positions, with closed limbs. After posing, the participants engaged in a gambling study to assess their willingness to take risks; in addition, their saliva was tested for changes in the levels of the hormones testosterone and cortisol.

In humans and other animals, testosterone levels both reflect and reinforce status and dominance. One might speculate that testosterone levels in brass musicians are already high enough, but for an individual entering the stage, or an audition venue, there is a lot to be said for feeling confident and eager to take risks—both characteristics that are boosted by testosterone. In contrast, cortisol is one of the body's stress hormones, and prolonged exposure to it interferes negatively with memory, learning and the immune system—not something you want too much of when already in a high-stress environment such as a classical music performance.

The results were very interesting: high-power posers exhibited an increase in testosterone and a decrease in cortisol, whereas low-power posers exhibited the opposite. Furthermore, high-power posers were more likely than low-power posers to focus on rewards, and showed a greater tolerance for risk. Finally, high-power posers reported feeling significantly more "powerful" and "in charge" than low-power posers did. The researchers concluded, "Thus, a simple 2-min power-pose manipulation was enough to significantly alter the physiological, mental, and feeling states of our participants. The implications of these results for everyday life are substantial."[26]

---

[26] It should be noted that the findings are being debated, as another team has failed to replicate the original study. Ranehill, E. et al. Assessing the robustness of power posing: no effect on hormones and risk tolerance in a large sample of men and women. *Psychological Science* **26**, 653-656 (2015).

## Psychology of breathing

Knowing about the different processes involved in breathing, what muscles are involved, and a bit of basic physics is beneficial for a general understanding of how our body functions during wind instrument playing. But it is difficult to control these processes directly, as the level of detail that would be required to organize and communicate with all the different muscles is probably beyond the abilities of the conscious brain. First, the sensory feedback that we get from the respiratory muscles is very superficial and coarse, compared to that from other parts of the body used for playing musical instruments, such as our fingers and lips. The diaphragm, which is so important for breathing, conveys almost no information about its position, or degree of contraction, to conscious levels of the brain. Instead, most of what we feel is the displacement of other tissues and the surrounding muscles.

Even with a correct understanding of the muscle movements involved in breathing, as described above, we can order only the illusion of breathing. By moving the abdominal and chest areas, we get what we order: shape changes of the torso. But we do not get breathing—there is not necessarily any air going in or out. Jacobs referred to this as "pseudo-expansion and compression of the lungs". Yet, most of the time, when we do not think about breathing (for example when we are sleeping, or focused on something else), it happens naturally and automatically. This is the big paradox: the more we are aware of our breathing, and try to control it, the more artificial it becomes. This is why we need to understand the psychology of breathing—how to think the thoughts that will tell the body what to do, without getting our consciousness involved in trying to control functions that are better carried out by lower levels of the brain. Much of our conscious, volitional thinking takes place in the frontal lobes of the brain, whereas many automatic processes, which we share with animals much lower on the evolutionary tree, are governed by a more primitive region at the base of the brain, called the brainstem. Breathing, when we leave it alone, is one of these automatic processes.

Instead of ordering contractions of the respiratory muscles, we can order the desired end product with the conscious part of the brain, and let the part of the brain connected to the muscles figure out how to instruct them. Arnold Jacobs used the phrase, "Don't expand to breathe; breathe to expand." So if we order air to come into the mouth, by thinking of sucking in air with minimal friction, this simple thought will trigger the more complicated task of contracting the right muscles—the diaphragm and external intercostals—to expand the lungs. Similarly, when we want to reverse the airstream and blow out, we just have to order wind at the lips, and the brain will organize the muscles needed to achieve this end product—in this case, deactivating the diaphragm and the external intercostals, and activating the abdominal muscles and the internal intercostals. All the time, however, the mental focus is on the air entering and leaving the mouth.

### *Inhalation*

If we think of sucking in air at the lips, we can strengthen this experience by involving other senses. Specifically, we can use our lips' sense of touch to feel the air passing between them, and we can use our sense of hearing to listen for the sound of air entering the mouth with minimal friction. Simply by pronouncing the syllable "WOH" when breathing in, one can take care of several important aspects of technique. The W in WOH makes a relaxed opening between the lips, while the O ensures that the tongue stays low, and out of the way of the airstream. Both of these conditions minimize the friction encountered by air entering and passing through the mouth. Moreover, with the WOH syllable, one feels the air near the front of the mouth, instead of back in the throat, as would be the case for a yawn, with the syllable "HA". This would make the opening of the mouth larger than the diameter of the windpipe (trachea), which is only 25 millimeters. When this happens, we get a bottleneck phenomenon—a sort of traffic jam of air that creates more friction at the entrance to the throat.

The most efficient way for a trumpet player or horn player to breathe is with a puckered embouchure, as described in the previous chapter, and the WOH-breath. With the mouthpiece rim remaining on the lips, simply relax the corners of the embouchure and inhale, allowing air to enter at the sides of the mouth. As we have seen, there is nothing to be gained by opening the mouth more widely, because of the bottleneck at the throat. Moreover, if one is constantly removing the mouthpiece and opening the mouth to breathe, there will always be the danger that the lips are not sufficiently close together, ready to vibrate inside the rim for the first notes after the breath. When breathing through the corners, it is important to avoid stretching the lips into a smile, as this thins the lips in the center. It can also restrict the openings at the sides, limiting the inward airflow, and making the breath noisy.

To experience how much air can be taken in through relaxed corners, try this little experiment. Take a drinking straw (about 7 mm in diameter) and cut it into three pieces of equal length. Place one of these short straws between the lips and breathe in and out through it, to establish a natural way of breathing through a small space. Then try using two straws at once, which will halve the time needed to take in the same amount of air. It will be even faster with three straws. Then place the straws in the corner of the mouth, and feel how much air can be taken in there by relaxing the corners, without disturbing the lips in the center.

Some methods advocate tight corners even when breathing in, but this creates more friction for the breath. As a consequence, less air is taken in, and the constant contraction of corners will tire the muscles unnecessarily. The combination of these two factors can cause stamina problems. The puckered embouchure is a nice cushion for the mouthpiece, more lip mass is inside the rim of the mouthpiece, available for buzzing when needed, and the playing and breathing positions are very similar. This can be crucial for players who prefer not to have time between inhalation and exhalation, but instead want to play immediately after breathing in, without any hesitation. Hesitation can trigger the diaphragm and abdominal muscles to work against each other, as described earlier, which is of course detrimental for playing. This effect is not universal, however: other players are able to stay relaxed, even when waiting a little after the breath.[27]

Depending on the size of their mouths, trombonists and tubists may have to either drop the jaw or engage in a smile-like movement for breathing. This is not such a problem for them, as the vibrating area of their lips is most often significantly larger than in trumpet or horn embouchures. As a

---

[27] The app "Poper's Game", by Joel Brennan, addresses this problem of hesitation before attacking a note after a breath.

consequence, these low-brass players do not need to gather their lips after a breath in the same way as high-brass players do, especially before a high note.

The student can practice inhaling with the WOH-breath by using a finger placed on the mouth, instead of a mouthpiece—to get used to being able to breathe with something placed on the lips. At the end of this chapter, we will describe breathing exercises to improve the fullness and speed of these breaths.

Occasionally, students are told to breathe quietly. This advice is probably given primarily to avoid unnecessary friction, but air entering the mouth, especially if it is a fast breath, will make some noise. A quiet breath may just be a pseudo-breath, where the student opens the mouth and tries to expand the chest and abdomen, but no air is taken in. The WOH-breath with relaxed corners is very efficient and makes very little noise, but is not completely silent.

### Exhalation

Some players do not have to think much about blowing. For them, releasing the breath into the instrument is so easy that it feels like doing nothing. Other players have to think explicitly about blowing wind at the lips, to be sure of providing enough aerodynamic energy to make a good sound.

As discussed earlier, the muscles responsible for blowing also take part in other, unrelated tasks that involve generating pelvic pressure; so, beyond engaging these muscles, the player must also stimulate the act of blowing—that is, wind moving at the lips, where it is needed to make them vibrate. The moving airstream, the wind, has to be ordered psychologically, to engage neurons to trigger the appropriate muscular function to move air to the lips. The player can do this by thinking about blowing air through the horn, blowing to the end of the concert hall, moving a little sailboat, blowing out candles on a birthday cake, or any other thought that will trigger the wind to be expelled for vibration of the lips. As we have discussed, air is in fact needed only at the lips, not in the instrument or to carry the sound into the hall. Nevertheless, these images of far-travelling air have the desired effect of triggering wind at the lips.

If a student has trouble using air freely, it may help to remove the instrument, as this may be a source of unhelpful conditioned reflexes. (Again, neurons that fire together, wire together.) If he is tensing muscles counterproductively, then taking away the trigger for this habit, the instrument, and just blowing wind, can be an efficient way to establish healthier habits. In particular, he can rehearse wind patterns: releasing air from lips formed into an embouchure, using the rhythm and articulation of whatever music is being rehearsed. When he returns to the instrument, some of the newly rehearsed way of blowing should appear in the playing, sometimes with dramatic effect. Practicing wind patterns is mostly useful for wind and articulation, but it can also help to improve embouchure formation. If a student plays with lips that are too tight (which is most often the case), she can practice wind patterns with a loose embouchure to relax the lips, experience greater airflow ("thick" air), and open up the sound. Conversely, a student who normally plays with lips that are too loose can practice wind patterns with a firmer embouchure.

When blowing wind patterns, it is important to emphasize the air going to—and past—the lips, and de-emphasize the involvement of the tongue. In playing, every time the tongue closes off the airstream, the lips cannot buzz and there is momentary silence. It is accordingly important to minimize these interruptions. It is also helpful to involve other senses to strengthen one's relationship with the air, as it is difficult to feel what the air is doing inside the body. Blowing wind patterns on the back of the hand makes the player aware of the airstream, and triggers correct blowing. There is also a sound associated with greater airflow, as well as the possibility of coupling the experience of blowing with the visual sense by using breathing equipment, as will be discussed below.

Wind patterns should be close simulations of the music. Passages in the low range should be patterned with a relaxed embouchure and large flow, whereas those in the high range call for a firmer embouchure and more air pressure. Wind patterns for loud playing should be performed using fast air, those for soft playing with slower air. The player should always be hearing the music in his head while performing the wind patterns.

The utility of practicing wind patterns will depend on the needs of the individual student. One who makes a great sound throughout her range evidently does not need this help, as she must already be providing sufficient air to her embouchure. But for the student who has problems with blowing freely, the frequent practice of wind patterns can have a striking effect on his playing.

If, after having worked with wind patterns for some time, a student is still holding back the breath, she may have strong conditioned reflexes that need a little more freeing up. The most common of these, because of the widespread tight-gut method, is the maintenance of a downward-contracted diaphragm during exhalation, leading to the immobilization of the abdominal region. To overcome this problem, the teacher can suggest that the student practice pulling in the abdomen when blowing. This pulling-in can happen only if the diaphragm relaxes upward, thereby stimulating the proper function. A student who has learned the habit of contracting the diaphragm while blowing will, at first, need to exaggerate the upward movement of the deactivated and relaxed diaphragm as he starts to blow. The diaphragm moves down when breathing in, and the abdomen comes in when blowing out. The student can encourage the appropriate movements by placing a hand on his abdomen, to feel these movements when breathing in and out. This can also be done during mouthpiece playing, when the student has one hand free. The correct movements may feel very strange to a student who has developed a strong habit of abdominal immobilization, but it can make a huge positive change to one's playing to have the power of a full breath available, instead of just what can be provided by compression in the chest. The proper use of the diaphragm and abdominal muscles can improve a player's sound quality, upper-register playing, use of dynamics and articulation—in other words, the basic foundations of playing a wind instrument. Physiologically, the student is changing from compressing the intestines to compressing the lungs, which indeed makes much more sense for a wind player.

### *H-consonants*
Ordering and stimulating a big, beautiful, free sound and thick, abundant airflow at the lips, while pulling in the belly, are all working in the direction of freeing up the breath; and there is one more technique to discuss in this connection. When we pronounce the H-consonant in speech, it triggers moderate contraction of the abdominal muscles and

relaxation of the diaphragm. As this is a reflex that we have already developed in learning to speak, all we need to do is apply it to our playing.

We will return to consonants in the next chapter, but what is relevant here is that emphasizing the H when beginning a note will help to ensure that air is moving freely to the lips. Using a clear T and almost simultaneously the H-consonant and O-vowel, can free up the air's passage to the lips. The tongue quickly gets out of the way with the T, air is released with the H, and the tongue stays down with the O, as the tone continues. All of this can happen by just thinking tHO. (We notate this articulation with a lower-case t, to show that the tongue gets quickly out of the way and is de-emphasized).

Using the H-consonant causes air to be released quickly, producing a note that starts relatively loud, followed by a diminuendo—in other words, a bell accent. The H-consonant provides an efficient and relaxed way of producing bell accents, which makes it easy for a player to add excitement to her playing, with minimal effort. H-consonants can also be used when accents are called for in legato playing. Most brass players play the Herbert Clarke Technical Studies as one smooth legato exercise, neglecting the fact that most of the exercises are written with two to four accents in each bar. If a player starts to play these accents using H-consonants, whether in legato or staccato, he will usually free up the breath, achieving easier tone production with better sound. Furthermore, as we will see when we come to discuss articulation, this is another example of a great tool for making complex muscular functions occur with a simple thought. tHO becomes a part of the song in the head, and the brain carries out the instruction automatically by precisely signaling and organizing the appropriate muscles.

## Breathing equipment

String players are fortunate to be able to observe the operation of their instrument with the two strongest human senses: those of touch and sight. As brass players, we can discern very little of what is going on when we play, as the required actions happen mostly inside the body. This is probably the main reason why misconceptions about breathing flourish in methodologies pertaining to wind playing; there are severe limits to what we can learn from seeing and feeling, while playing a wind instrument.

Arnold Jacobs addressed this problem by introducing into brass pedagogy breathing machines,[28] which can allow respiratory functions to be monitored with the visual sense. All of these machines have an object, such as a ball or a meter, that moves in response to the movement of air. As a student blows air with different amounts of pressure or flow, he can monitor and change his breathing patterns, and then apply what he has learned to playing the instrument. Often, these machines are thought of as ways to build strength and respiratory muscle, but this is not their real benefit. Instead, their contribution is more psychological in nature, in that they give the student an opportunity to "see" the air, or more accurately the effect of air movement. With different challenges created by various settings of the machines, the subconscious brain will try to meet those challenges in the most efficient way. The machines react only to the air that is blown, not to how much effort is exerted. Recall that air is moved out of the lungs partly by relaxing the inspiratory muscles, allowing the elasticity of lungs and rib cage to come into play, and partly by contracting the expiratory muscles. This requires less muscular effort than when the inspiratory and expiratory muscles are fighting each other. By removing the trigger of conditioned reflexes, namely the instrument, and being able to "see" the wind, the student will be able to establish helpful new habits. In other words, the machine will react objectively to the product of the respiratory apparatus, not to how the student feels.

### The Breath Builder

The Breath Builder is a cylinder containing a ping-pong ball, which can be kept at the top of the cylinder by a sufficient flow of air—either in or out. As a student alternates between inhaling and exhaling, with breaths lasting as long as possible, she will find a way to minimize muscular effort. She will also learn how to take full breaths without thinking about where to place the air in the body. As long as she is breathing in, the ball must stay up, and the same applies when blowing out. The brain will

---

[28] An instructional video demonstrating breathing exercises and the use of breathing equipment can be downloaded at https://www.playwithapro.com/video/kristian-steenstrup-breathing-fundamentals-with-kr.

subconsciously engage the correct muscles to satisfy these demands, in response to the conscious focus on keeping the ball aloft. The machine also trains the ability to breathe in and blow out without hesitation, as constant air movement is required to keep the ball from falling down. Small holes in the top of the cylinder make it possible to simulate the different resistances imposed on the airflow by the embouchure, according to the register. The more holes that are open, the less resistance and the lower the range represented. It is good to start with all holes open, and then experience the increased effort required to keep the ball up as more holes are covered, as if moving into the higher range. During inhalation, the holes should always stay open, as no resistance is necessary here.

Articulations can also be added, to check that the airflow is not cut off by the tongue.

### *The Breathing Bag*
The Breathing Bag is a rubber bladder, with a typical maximum volume of 4–6 liters of air. The student should first take a full breath and fill the bag with air, then breathe in and out repeatedly, with the mouth of the bag remaining on the lips. The visible inflation and deflation of the bag provides a visual cue that air is moving, ensuring that the student isn't taking pseudo-breaths. Because the student re-breathes the same air (containing carbon dioxide), there is no danger of hyperventilation. He can also do wind patterns, ensuring constant airflow by monitoring the expansion of the bag, and full inhalations by its deflation. One can also attach a mouthpiece to the bag, to monitor constant airflow while playing.

If a student has the habit of taking breaths that are too shallow, he can bypass it by filling the bag, taking a full breath from it, and using this breath to play the instrument. It is a little cumbersome, but can make a big difference if the student is not used to playing with full breaths.

### *The Incentive Spirometer*
Like the Breath Builder, the Incentive Spirometer also has a small ball that can be raised to the top of a tube by airflow. It was originally designed to give a visual demonstration of inhalation, but can be used for exhalation by turning it upside down. It has different settings, making it possible to simulate the resistances of different instruments and ranges. One can also

remove the flexible tube, and instead apply a funnel, such as the stem from a trumpet harmon mute, and perform wind patterns into this, setting up different challenges by changing the resistance.

It is also possible to attach a mouthpiece to the spirometer, making it possible to stimulate good blowing while buzzing.

### The Variable Resistance Compound Gauge

Jacobs created the Variable Resistance Compound Gauge by attaching a tube with holes to a manometer. This makes it possible to simulate a wide range of air pressure, as required to play various instruments in different registers. High pressure, as demanded by the oboe, or by high playing on the trumpet, is particularly difficult to simulate using other breathing equipment, but easily done with this device.

## Breathing exercises

These exercises were developed by Arnold Jacobs, and should be practiced daily for months, and preferably years, to make full breathing a habit. The aim is to learn to inhale large volumes of air with minimal effort, and quickly. Many brass players do these exercises as part of a warm-up routine, as they stimulate the efficient use of air that is essential for brass playing; this can have the effect of shortening the time needed to warm up on the instrument. But the exercises do not have to be done in the morning; in fact, repeating them throughout the day can be beneficial, especially for students who are working to change their breathing habits.

1. The first exercise is based on long inhalation and exhalation: inhale over five slow beats, and then exhale over five slow beats. So the pattern is inhalation: 1 2 3 4 5, immediately followed by exhalation: 5 4 3 2 1.

   This exercise may also be done with accompanying arm movements: raising the arms progressively above the head during inhalation, keeping them there during exhalation, and returning them to your sides before the next inhalation. This helps to open the chest during inhalation, and because the diaphragm is attached to the sternum, it will be in its upward, relaxed position during exhalation.

2. Imagine the lung capacity as divided into thirds, so there is 3/3, 2/3, 1/3 or 0/3 of the full capacity of air in the lungs. Use the arm as a visual aid, so your hand is furthest away from the body at 0/3 and touches the lips at 3/3. Practice changing rapidly among these four settings.
3. Using 5/4 time, blow out on the first four quarter notes, and breathe in on the fifth quarter note.
4. The same principle, but in 4/4: blow out on the first seven eighth notes, and breathe in on the last eighth.
5. Blow out on the first 11 triplet eighth notes in 4/4 time, and breathe in on the last triplet eighth.
6. Blow out on the first 15 sixteenth notes in 4/4 time, and breathe in on the last sixteenth.

These exercises can also be practiced using the Breathing Bag, to add visual cues and avoid hyperventilation.

Exercises 3–6 can easily be adapted to playing the instrument, by substituting playing a single tone for blowing out. Practice using the WOH-breath while keeping the mouthpiece on the lips and relaxing the corners, so the first attack after the breath is easy. Make sure there is no hesitation, so the breath is always either going in or going out. In particular, there is no need to stop the air to set the embouchure, since it remains in place in the center of the mouthpiece.

## THE TONGUE

As a brass student works on developing her articulation technique, she can easily become caught up in trying to control the tongue's complex movements by consciously placing it in certain places in the mouth, according to whatever rules or methods she has been taught. Just as we have seen with the embouchure and breathing, ideas about the tongue's role in articulation are plentiful, and often apparently contradictory, making it difficult to know what to do.

Part of the problem with trying to devise explicit rules about the use of the tongue is that our tongues and oral cavities are all different in size and shape. More importantly, humans already have a refined control of the tongue, learned and incorporated since early childhood, because of the tongue's use in speech. Most adolescents and adults can speak fluently, and produce highly complicated speech sounds, simply by ordering a verbal message, without any conscious control of the tongue and lips. Furthermore, when a child learns to speak, he does it by listening to and imitating the sounds he hears, not by following instructions for correct tongue positions and movements.

In the same way, it is more fruitful for a brass student to train her tongue by doing diction exercises, rather than the more artificial and clumsy alternative of trying to control the muscles directly. The mind controls the speech (in this case, certain syllables), and the reflexes of speech control the tongue. This brings us back again to controlling the song. The performer can mentally sing the syllables that she wishes to apply in her playing, and the brain will send neural signals to the tongue so it performs the required maneuvers. A great way to establish this habit is first to sing out loud the music one is rehearsing—with the proper pitch and rhythm, and now also with the desired syllables. Usually these syllables will be much easier to pronounce than those that the student speaks flawlessly every day in his language; a wind player will typically use relatively few and simple syllables, such as TA, TO, TEE, TA KA TA KA, TA TA KA, and so on.

## The consonant

The consonants used in brass playing are unvoiced, and have very little sound that can be separated from the start of the subsequent vowel. When we pronounce the word TALK, we do not hear the T before it is over, which is when the vowel A starts to be heard. To produce the T, the tongue briefly closes off the air passage, then opens it again as it moves down to pronounce the vowel. This is also what happens when we articulate on a wind instrument. It is the downward motion of the tongue that allows air to pass to the lips, so they can vibrate. The closure of the mouth cavity by the tongue, making the consonant, ideally interrupts the airstream only for a very short time, since the lips need the air to vibrate. It can create serious problems for a brass player if he thinks of the upward movement of the tongue as what starts the note. The more he closes off the airstream with the tongue's upward movement, the longer the delay before air passes to the lips. Delaying the start of the note in this way can lead to an accumulation of air pressure behind the tongue. When the tongue finally goes down, this pressure will be released with an explosive effect, giving the start of the note an unpleasant, forced sound.

To develop clear articulation, the brass player can use the T as it is pronounced in English, as this is a very short and clear consonant. The tongue ideally gets out of the way very quickly, allowing an immediate transition to the vowel—that is, the passage of air, and production of the note. It is important not to over-emphasize the T, or any other hard consonant used to start a note, as this can easily lead to closure of the air passage. By contrast, adding an H-consonant, as discussed in the previous chapter, emphasizes the flow of air, and leads to less resistance to this flow. Starting to think of clear articulation as comprising a small, clear T, an aspirated H, and a low vowel O (tHO) allows for uninterrupted, fluent articulation and tone production.

Usually, the English T is pronounced by the tongue moving up and down in the mouth, often contacting the roof of the mouth near the ridge behind the teeth. Frequently, however, brass players articulate with their tongues quite far forward in the mouth: between the teeth, or even between the lips. This means that the tongue needs to travel back and forth, instead of up and down. This back and forth motion can be quite clumsy, and—especially in multiple tonguing, when the TA syllable has to alternate with the back of the tongue pronouncing KA—the tongue may obstruct the airstream longer than is necessary. Doing diction exercises away from the instrument can help a player find the most efficient articulation. First, she can pronounce the syllable LA several times (ALALALALALA….), feeling the easy up and down movement of the tongue; and then introduce the TA syllable (ALATA, ALATATA, ALATATATA….), imitating this easy movement. Training diction in this way should help to free up the tongue, and make it more nimble.

For students who did not grow up in English-speaking countries, the clear English T may not be part of their language. This can be addressed by giving the student diction exercises in which he is asked to imitate the clear speech of the teacher. A student who can learn to pronounce words and sentences such as, "It's time to talk Turkish", "twenty-two" and "it's twenty-two to two", will soon be able to use this clear T in his own playing.

Once a student has mastered the basic skill of starting a note clearly, she can start to develop a wide vocabulary of different types of articulation. Between the softest D and the hardest T, there is a virtually unlimited range of clarity of attack. The really great players have amazing control over their articulations, from a very smooth legato tongue all the way to a hard sforzato accent, and use these as part of their musical expression. By listening to such players and building strong aural images of the sounds they produce, a student may get much further than by trying to control the tongue directly.

## The illusion of staccato

Often brass players will acquire the habit of playing staccato notes by stopping the note with a T, sometimes called a "tongue stop" or a "double-consonant". When a player uses this technique to play several articulated notes consecutively in a relative fast tempo (TAT-TAT-TAT…), the tongue will shut off the airstream more than is necessary. This will impair the tone quality, and soon the player will experience stamina problems, as the lips are being starved of air. Over-using the tongue in this way will also cause it to become quite stiff, limiting its speed. This is normally not a desirable way to articulate in classical music, but is occasionally employed in certain types of commercial music.

At a slow tempo, one does need to stop the airstream to play staccato, but this can be done by simply ceasing to blow, rather than stopping the air with the tongue. At faster tempos, however, it is possible to create the illusion of staccato without in fact stopping the airstream. If a player plays a fast stream of long notes, starting each note with a D articulation, they will sound tenuto. But if he starts each note with a clear T, the same stream of notes will sound staccato. The clearness of articulation at the beginning of each note will make the note start a little louder, and then decay in volume. At a fast tempo, this decay will fool the ear into perceiving space between the notes, even though there is no actual silence. The notes sound staccato, but the tongue can move easily, air is not being shut off on each note, the sound is better, and there will not be stamina problems caused by blocking the flow of air to the lips.

This technique can be developed by playing the articulated passage first slowly in legato. Focus on good quality of sound, good airflow to the lips, and no involvement of the tongue at all. Then, still at the slow tempo, add the tongue, but keep the notes long and sustained, with no space between them: quasi-legato. Then start applying clear, English T's (as in "twenty-two"), while still emphasizing the vowel, rather than the consonant—as if you were saying tO, tO, tO. Then you can start gradually increasing the tempo, while maintaining good connection between the notes. This technique can be practiced using scales, the Herbert Clarke Technical Studies, exercises from Arban's book, or any musical passage. A relaxed articulation is even more important when using multiple tonguing, as such passages are invariably fast, requiring the tongue to be flexible and fluent.

## The vowel

In speech, vowels take up most of the time needed to say most words. In singing, which is quite analogous to brass playing, they can be even more extended. The consonant is just a way of getting into the note; the vowel sustains the sound. The vowel segment of the brass player's syllable is also when air can flow easily to the lips, as it is not being blocked by the tongue. To allow air to pass as freely as possible to the lips, with minimal interruption to the airstream, or loss of energy to friction, it makes sense to use the vowel that keeps the tongue as low as possible in the mouth, namely O.

Another argument for a low tongue position comes from its effect on timbre and intonation, with a lower tongue yielding a "rounder" sound and lower intonation.[29] This is due to the interaction of the air column of the instrument with the air in the player's vocal tract, during the opening phase of the lips' vibratory cycles.[30]

Many methods for brass players and pedagogues advocate the use of different vowels as a primary means of controlling pitch. Typically, a low-tongue vowel such as O or AH is used in the low range, with a succession of higher-tongue vowels, and a progressively higher tongue arch, used for ascending into higher registers. By contrast, Arnold Jacobs recommended keeping a relatively low tongue position, except in the extreme high range, reserving the tongue primarily for applying color changes, rather than changing the pitch. Jacobs felt that trumpet players, especially, were liable to use too high a tongue position in the low to moderately high range, leading to more resistance to the air stream, thinner sound, limitations in the louder dynamics, and stamina problems.

The usual argument for raising the back of the tongue when ascending into the high range is to increase the air speed. It is true that air moves more quickly between the lips when playing higher notes, as the higher vibration rate requires the lips to be more tense and/or stiffer —either of which will be associated with higher air speed. It is also true that, when we raise the back of the tongue, air will flow faster through the constricted passage between the arch of the tongue and the roof of the mouth, as described by the Bernoulli principle. (This is, in fact, a specific application of the principle, known as the Venturi effect.) But the problem is that the passage immediately after the back of the tongue widens, so the air speed will go down again before the air reaches the lips. Not only will the player

---

29  Wolfe, J. et al. Some effects of the player's vocal tract and tongue on wind instrument sound. *Proceedings of the Stockholm Music Acoustics Conference*, August 6–9, 2003 (SMAC 03). In experiments using an artificial lip-reed player attached to a trombone, a simplified vocal tract modelling a raised tongue position produced a thinner sound, with pitch raised by about a fifth of a half-tone, compared with the sound produced by a tract modelling a low tongue.
30  Peterson, Ben. *Trumpet Science: Understanding Performance Through Physics, Physiology, and Psychology* (Peterson Music, 2012), p. 42.

have gained nothing in air speed, but the air may in fact have lost energy because of increased friction in the constricted passage. Moreover, as mentioned above, the sound quality may suffer, owing to the reduced size of the vocal tract caused by the tongue position.

One can experience the lack of effect of tongue position on air speed with a simple experiment. Blow a steady airstream onto your hand, using an O-vowel, and then raise the tongue into an E-vowel. You will not feel any increase in air speed.

Sometimes a garden hose is used as a metaphor for what happens to air inside the mouth. If the diameter of the hose is reduced at its end, as with a nozzle, the water will indeed flow faster. But with the E-vowel, this reduction happens several centimeters behind the lips. Making an obstruction in the garden hose around the same distance from its end will decrease the flow of water, not increase it.

Frequently, the use of tongue position to control pitch is linked to the phenomenon of whistling. In whistling, the mouth and tongue are the entire instrument, so the pitch is controlled by the tongue changing the size of the vocal tract, and hence its resonance frequency. This is analogous to changing the pitch of a brass instrument by altering the length of the tube. While, in principle, one might imagine that changing the resonance of the vocal tract could affect the pitch of the entire system (vocal tract plus instrument), in fact it doesn't seem that this effect is important throughout most of the normal range of classical trumpet playing[31]. Indeed, experiments on seven trumpet players showed that the subjects did not systematically tune their vocal tract resonances "for normal playing, high note playing, or during pitch bending."[32] They played notes as high as F6 (written G6 on the Bb trumpet) without having to tune their vocal tracts—in other words, without using the tongue to

---

31   In technical terms, below a frequency of about 1 kHz (around C#6 on the Bb trumpet), the resonance peaks in the impedance spectrum of the vocal tract are significantly smaller than those for the bore of the instrument, so the acoustical properties of the instrument will dominate. See Chen et al. (2012), cited below.
32   Chen, Jer-Ming et al. Do trumpet players tune resonances of the vocal tract? *Journal of the Acoustical Society of America* **131**, 722-727 (2012).

facilitate playing in the high range. The researchers concluded that, whereas saxophone players cannot play in their uppermost register without tuning their tract resonances, trumpet players can get away without this technique (at least, up to F6) because they have greater control over the vibrating reed—in their case, the lips—and probably also adjust the amount of air pressure in the mouth.

In an earlier study,[33] Jody Hall X-rayed the mouths of nine trumpet players as they played Bb3, Bb4 and Bb5. He found that, when the players moved from the middle register into the high register, their most frequent tendencies were to raise the lower jaw, move the high point of the tongue forward and downward, and enlarge the throat cavity. He also found that the position of the tongue affected sound quality more than anything else.

In an additional high-note experiment, three players were examined while playing E6. All three moved their tongues to "ee"-positions for these notes, leading Hall to conclude that, somewhere in the extremely high register, it becomes necessary to place the tongue in this position.

As a result of his investigations, Hall developed several concepts for his teaching:

1. *A tone quality which is consistent in all registers should be the controlling factor in determining basic tongue position.*

2. *In order to develop a consistent tone quality in all registers, emphasis should be placed on changing register by use of the embouchure and breath support alone (without aid from the tongue).*[34]

3. *If the "ah-ee" change is ever used with inexperienced students as a device to aid in register change, it should be done with an awareness that eventually that method will be altered or abandoned.*

---

[33]   Hall, Jody C. To "Ah-ee" or not to "Ah-ee". *The Instrumentalist*, April 1955. Reprinted in *Brass Anthology: A Collection of Brass Articles Published in the Instrumentalist Magazine from 1946 to 1986* (Instrumentalist Co., **1987**), pp. 173-174.

[34]   Consistent with the findings in Chen et al. (2012), cited above.

4. *After advanced students have learned to play in all registers with one basic tongue position and tone quality, they can learn to produce different qualities of tone, as demanded by the music, by varying the tongue position.*

## Using the Venturi effect

Although, as discussed above, the Venturi effect caused by the raised arch of the tongue seems incapable of increasing the speed of the air reaching the lips, a variation of it may yield the desired result. If the tongue can combine with the mouth cavity to act as a funnel, delivering air to the embouchure with no widening of the passage, there will be no deceleration of the airstream, and the embouchure will indeed act as a nozzle. This can serve as a plausible way to increase air speed, if the player can gain control over the tongue to direct the air to the lips, particularly in the extreme high range of the trumpet. This may be what some lead trumpet players are doing with great success.

As previously discussed, however, reducing the size of the vocal tract—in this case, by quite a bit—comes at the price of a thinner sound. It would therefore seem sensible for classical trumpet players, at least, to reserve this raised-tongue technique for the extreme high range, above E6. This range is not used much in classical music, and the notes up there are so high in the harmonic series that they have very few overtones in any case, so the price for narrowing the vocal tract is not big in this range. The air speed needed to play in the high range mainly comes from the respiratory system, but it is handy to be able to use the Venturi-tongue for extreme high playing. Unfortunately, classical brass students are often taught to start raising the tongue (constricting the vocal tract) in the middle register, making it difficult for them to maintain good sound quality throughout their range.

## ZEN AND THE ART OF EMBOUCHURE MAINTENANCE

Despite his vast knowledge of the mechanics of brass playing, Arnold Jacobs in his teaching constantly emphasized the importance of letting go of this information, and trusting the brain and body to coordinate and execute the complex motor skills required to perform on a brass instrument. The understanding of the inner workings is important for the teacher, who needs to analyze the students, but for the performer this can lead to self-analysis, "paralysis by analysis", tentativeness and self-doubt. A performer who is also a teacher must be able to shift between these two modes of thinking, in order to function optimally.

The dichotomy between being conscious of the complicated workings of the human body and brain, as a teacher, and letting go of this information as a performer, finds an echo in ideas and findings in neuroscience, psychology and athletic performance in the second half of the 20th century.

The research of the Nobel laureate Roger W. Sperry led to theories of lateralization of the brain hemispheres, which have served as a functional model for this phenomenon in popular psychology. According to this view, the two halves of the brain function very differently from one another, each of them specializing in different tasks. The left hemisphere is responsible for analytical tasks, such as cognitive learning; it is critical, works with technique and thinks linearly. Its thinking is limited to two alternatives, such as yes/no or black/white, and movements under its control seem robotic and forced. By contrast, the right hemisphere works with sounds, images and feelings. Learning happens aurally, visually and kinesthetically. The right brain is creative and artistic, and very much involved with the imagination, which can work with infinite possibilities. Its thinking is holistic, and it generates natural, flowing movements. Successful performers know the feeling of letting go and being in the present moment—ceding control to the right brain, and trusting its quiet competence.[35]

The terminology of left and right brain is well established in the realm of sports and performance psychology, but recent research in neuroscience suggests that this description oversimplifies the way the brain works.[36] It now seems that the two halves of the brain are in constant communication with each other—making it difficult to identify, for example, creative processes as being dominantly right-brain rather than left-brain. Nevertheless, the idea that the brain has two modes of operation, predominantly analytical or artistic, provides a useful model for working with the mind to achieve optimal performance.

A classic work in sports psychology, diligently employed by musicians, Timothy Gallwey's *The Inner Game of Tennis*[37] presents a more scientifically neutral yet very useful terminology, naming the two modes or levels of mind, "Self 1" and "Self 2". Self 1 is the conscious teller, and Self 2 the subconscious doer. Self 1, the conscious brain, tends to over-control everything, not trusting the competence of Self 2, the body, to do its job. (One adverse consequence of such over-control can be excessive muscle tension.) Self 1 is the ego-mind, the human inclination to judge and control everything; but for peak performance, in both athletics and music, Self 1 has to let go, lose control, and delegate to levels of the brain that know how to coordinate the complex muscle groups responsible for refined physical skills.

---

35   Greene, Don. *Performance Mastery: Reach Your Peak* (2013). E-book, available at http://dongreene.com/live/shop/performance-mastery-reach-your-peak/.
36   Kosslyn, Stephen M. & Miller, G. Wayne. *Top Brain, Bottom Brain*, (Simon & Schuster, 2nd edition, 2014): "So the hemispheres do differ, but at a more specific and detailed level than is claimed in the popular press and on the Internet. One half-brain is not 'logical' and the other 'intuitive,' nor is one more 'analytical' and the other more 'creative'. Both halves play important roles in logical and intuitive thinking, in analytical and creative thinking, and so forth. All of the popular distinctions involve complex functions, which are accomplished by multiple processes — some of which may operate better in the left hemisphere and some of which may operate better in the right hemisphere — but the overall functions cannot be said to be entirely the province of one or the other hemisphere."
37   Gallwey, Timothy. *The Inner Game of Tennis: The Ultimate Guide to the Mental Side of Peak Performance* (Pan Macmillan, 2015).

The contrast between ego-mind and letting go features prominently in the well known book *Zen in the Art of Archery*,[38] in which the German philosopher Eugen Herrigel (1884–1955) describes his years of study with a master—a *sensei*—of classic Japanese archery. The sensei encouraged Herrigel to "loose the shots"—that is, let go of the arrows, instead of satisfying the ego-mind by obsessing about hitting the target. In a similar way, brass players tend to worry about playing the first notes after silence, in fear of missing the notes or otherwise not living up to expectations. Often, the ego makes the player hold back, where letting go and trusting Self 2 to operate the embouchure, breath and tongue would be more successful.

For this reason, music teachers often find it fruitful to use words that will trigger Self 2, or the "right brain". Thus, instead of being given an explicit technical instruction—such as engaging specific muscles—a student may be invited to think of a desired sound, to evoke the appropriate activity in the mind. Arnold Jacobs would frequently ask the student to "sing in the brain", "flood your brain with sound", or "imagine a beautiful sound coming out of the bell", prompting a holistic approach to playing. For the "wind" aspect of playing, mental images such as "blow a little sailboat and watch it as you play", or "air should be like a fountain of water that comes up, and a rubber ball sits and floats; that's your tone," usually work well. Kinesthetic feelings are also in the domain of the "right brain", so Self 2 can be triggered by appealing to a sense of ease, air flowing without resistance, and a feeling of relaxation—generally, but also specifically in the lips, tongue and respiratory muscles. Engaging in imagination presents limitless possibilities for the creative, artistically interested student.

Finally, Self 1 demands quick results, whereas Self 2 loves to be in the process. This has obvious implications for practicing, where advanced students will often expect rapid improvement, in accordance with the quick-fix trends of modern society, as opposed to the patient cultivation of being in the process. In particular, students tend to expect their learning

---

38   Herrigel, Eugen. *Zen in the Art of Archery* (Pantheon Books, 1953).

trajectory to follow a straight line, trending continuously upwards, whereas in reality long-term learning happens as a series of steps and plateaus, with most of our time spent on the plateaus.[39][40] We must learn to love the plateaus, and cultivate practice for its own sake. As George Leonard, an American who studied the Japanese martial art aikido, writes in his book, *Mastery*, "How do you best move toward mastery? To put it simply, you practice diligently, but you practice primarily for the sake of the practice itself. Rather than being frustrated while on the plateau, you learn to appreciate and enjoy it just as much as you do the upward surges."

---

39    Leonard, George. *Mastery: The Keys to Success and Long-Term Fulfillment* (Plume, 1992).
40    Greene, Don. *11 Strategies for Audition and Performance Success* (2012). Workbook, available at http://psi.dongreene.com/wp-content/uploads/11Strategies.pdf.

## PRACTICING

Knowing how to practice is essential for improving our playing. Although lessons with a good teacher can open our eyes, and even help us to experience better and more enjoyable playing, it is the daily time spent working with our instrument—and the mental attitude that we bring to this work—that will bring about lasting changes, and our development as musicians.

Each instrument has longstanding traditions of learning, which can have quite robust rules regarding the best way to practice. In the realm of brass instruments, some traditions emphasize muscle building—developing strength, especially in the lip muscles—while others give priority to the respiratory aspects of wind playing. Still other schools of thought focus more on the musical output, and there are numerous methods, each promoting its preferred balance between musical values and physical aspects of playing. Countless exercises are available, often with no scientific rationale for their use, but supported by strong convictions that have taken generations to establish, and which would similarly take generations to abandon, if they were to prove ineffective.

Many of the brass methods established in the $20^{th}$ century fell into the trap of attempting to strengthen the different muscle groups responsible for sound production—those of the lip, tongue, respiratory system and fingers—without taking into account that none of these muscles can do anything without receiving signals from the brain. These signals have to be extremely precise, to exert the refined control necessary to play an instrument; moreover, the signals sent to the different destinations must be highly coordinated. Obviously, muscles are involved, and must be trained, but they will develop automatically, by playing the music that requires them. It accordingly makes more sense, when we seek to understand how humans learn physical skills, to start by looking at the brain. Music-making involves both cognitive learning and the acquiring of physical skills; in recent years, notable advances in both these realms have been made in the fields of neuroscience and educational and sports psychology, which are directly applicable to instrumental practice.[41]

## A myelin concerto

For decades, neuroscientists have wondered why it takes so long to become really good at something. Recently, some answers have begun to appear.

First, a bit of background. The average human brain has about 90 billion neurons.[42] This is a lot: it's about as many seconds as there are in 3,000 years. A neuron consists of a cell body, dendrites and an axon. Dendrites are small branches that extend out from the cell body and receive signals from other neurons; the axon, which splits into small branches at its end, conveys signals to other neurons. The terminal branches of one neuron's axon connect with another neuron's dendrites at junctions called synapses; each dendrite can have thousands of synapses. The electrical signal that travels down the axon can't cross the synapse; instead, the nerve impulse triggers the release of a chemical, known as a neurotransmitter. When the chemical signal reaching the synapse is large enough, it triggers an electrical signal in the receiving dendrite. Recalling that neurons have many dendrites, but only one axon, the receiving neuron responds to the sum of all the signals coming into it, which can come from up to 10,000 other neurons. If this sum crosses a certain threshold, the receiving neuron will "fire", transmitting a signal further down the line. A neuron either fires or it doesn't—an all-or-nothing function, analogous to the binary choice of 1 or 0 that underlies the functioning of digital computers. A sufficiently large stimulus can cause a cascade of signals to travel through a neural network, reminiscent of falling dominoes. All thoughts and mental processes, whether conscious or subconscious, are due to this basic process.

---

41    Kageyama, Noa. *Beyond practicing.* Online course, available at http://my.bulletproofmusician.com/beyond-practicing-2/.
42    Azevedo, Frederico A.C. et al. Equal numbers of neuronal and nonneuronal cells make the human brain an isometrically scaled-up primate brain. *Journal of Comparative Neurology* **513**, 532-541 (2009).

The brain has a tremendous potential to form new connections. With each of the 90 billion neurons having thousands of synaptic connections to other neurons, the average adult brain is estimated to have between 100 and 500 trillion synapses. When we have a new experience, a new thought, or perform a physical action, new dendrites may sprout and make contact to other neurons, forming new synapses.[43] Every thought we have is encoded by the firing of a specific group of neurons, all connected in a circuit. What is particularly interesting, when it comes to learning physical skills, is that when we repeat an action these synapses become stronger, meaning that the neural circuit becomes more effective.

This mechanism for learning, based on the strengthening of synaptic connections, has been understood for decades. More recently, however, a fatty substance called myelin has been implicated in the learning of motor skills. Myelin forms insulating sheaths around axons, which greatly increase the propagation speed of nerve impulses.[44] Myelin is produced and applied to axons by cells called oligodendrocytes—a subset of glial cells, which are non-neuronal cells that are as abundant as neurons in the human brain.

When we keep repeating the same action, more layers of myelin are wrapped around the axon, further increasing the communication speed. Thus, as we start learning to play a brass instrument, we can think of the neurons involved as being connected by the equivalent of a dial-up modem. Then, after thousands of hours of practice, the myelination of the axons in our brass-playing neural network will have upgraded it to broadband capacity. Messages will be transmitted speedily, and in well coordinated fashion, from the brain to our lip, tongue, respiratory and finger muscles, so they will operate in unison.

We begin to see how playing a brass instrument, or learning any other physical skill, is a consequence of physical changes in the brain caused by

---

43   Willis, Judy. *Research-Based Strategies to Ignite Student Learning: Insights from a Neurologist and Classroom Teacher* (Association for Supervision & Curriculum Development, 2007).
44   McKenzie, Ian A. et al. Motor skill learning requires active central myelination. *Science* 346, 318-322 (2014).

the repeated firing of neural circuits that instruct the muscles to perform actions that provide the desired results. As the coordinated firings of these neurons are repeated, and their connections become stronger and faster, they coordinate muscle groups splendidly and make us sound a certain way. Our brain changes with what we do, what we experience and what we repeat. If we spend hours every day, over a long period of time, sounding poor, we will myelinate and fortify the neural connections that are responsible for sounding that way; it will become the norm. We will become very good at sounding bad. Conversely, if we make a habit of sounding great, trying to imitate and compete with the most proficient musicians in the world, and repeat this for hours and hours, over months and years, we will make strong connections in the brain for sounding great. Sounding great becomes the norm, and we will find it strange to sound anything less than that again.

We can see, then, that practicing is not just about putting in lots of hours, doing lots of exercises and playing difficult music. There must also be an exacting discrimination between good and bad sounds, and between musical and less than musical playing.

This attitude needs to start with the warm-up. Students are occasionally heard warming up for an hour, running carelessly through lots of exercises and sounding mediocre. Then these same students expect to sound great when they have to play music. Starting with the first note we play, we need to try to sound our best. Every time we play a bad note, we are strengthening the neural circuit for that outcome, making it more likely that we will do it again. The same is true for good notes. Warming up should be a reinforcement of our best playing: starting with easy music, where we can maintain our highest standards, before moving on to more complicated music, with more challenges, and the potential for not sounding our best.

Arnold Jacobs often used the phrase, "you don't unlearn or fight a bad habit; you establish a new one," which makes even more sense when we understand how the brain changes physically as it executes our playing. We cannot dissolve the myelin that has already been laid down through many hours of practice, but we can use the brain's tremendous ability to form and strengthen new connections. As we start repeating a new habit, such as playing with a more beautiful sound, better intonation or minimal force, we are establishing a neural network that will reinforce the desired habit.

## Neurons that fire together, wire together

The process just described can be encapsulated in the principle, "Neurons that fire together, wire together". When we play the note A on the trumpet, for example, a neural circuit will fire to cause fingers one and two to depress the corresponding valves; another will start to establish itself, based on the sound of the note; a third will cause the lips to buzz with the appropriate frequency; a fourth will tell the respiratory muscles what to do; and, if we learn how this note is represented in written music, another circuit will fire to recognize this. As all these circuits fire simultaneously, the relevant neurons will begin to connect to each other and become part of the same circuit.[45]

When an experienced musician plays a wind instrument—assuming a habitual body posture, grasp of the instrument, use of the breathing muscles, tongue position and embouchure formation—the muscles responsible for all of these different but simultaneous actions are stimulated by circuits in the brain that are connected to each other and myelinated through years of practice. Changing your embouchure, breathing, sound, or any other aspect of your playing will be challenging, because each of these aspects is triggered into its habitual pattern by simply holding the instrument. This is why one of the most effective ways to change any playing habit is to remove the instrument temporarily, thereby freeing the other parts of your technique from their enslavement by the stimulus of holding the instrument. Singing the music, creating a mental aural image of sounding differently, working with the breath in wind patterns or with breathing equipment, and playing the mouthpiece are all ways of bypassing conditioned reflexes, and creating new connections in the brain that can help you to sound better and play with more ease. Usually, after employing one of these strategies, one can hear an improvement in a student's playing immediately after she

---

45   Gaertner, Tara. Cellular mechanisms of learning. http://trainingthemusicalbrain.blogspot.dk/2012/04/cellular-mechanisms-of-learning.html

returns to the instrument. But this improvement may last for only a few bars, as it easy for the old habits—preserved in the myelinated pathways and strengthened synapses established over many years—to reassert themselves. By repeating the cycle of relevant exercises without the instrument, followed immediately by playing the instrument, the student will strengthen the new habit, and be able to sustain the improved playing for longer, until eventually the old habit is replaced by the new one.

## Slow practice

From our earliest days of learning to play a musical instrument, we have probably all heard about the benefits of practicing slowly. To really gain from slow practice, it needs to be *really* slow: not just a few metronome markings under tempo, but slower than half-tempo, and perhaps even quarter-tempo, for particularly difficult passages. If we play this slowly and really observe the sound quality, and the connectivity of all the notes; make sure the air flows freely, and the fingers depress perfectly and sharply; ask for great intonation, clear articulation and unlimited other subtle degrees of excellence and flawlessness, we will ensure the establishment of neural connections that are responsible for all these qualities. As we repeat the passage at this high level of perfection—which is possible even for the most difficult passage, when playing extremely slowly—we will be adding myelin to the relevant circuits, improving the speed and coordination of neural signal transmission, which should allow us to play the passage accurately at much higher tempos. A few weeks of playing a passage very, very slowly is often sufficient to experience this phenomenon.

One widely used, and efficient, way to learn challenging fingerings on the trumpet, and other right-handed valve instruments, is to practice the combinations silently with the left hand. This technique probably owes its success to the fact that it forces the player to practice the fingerings very slowly, as most people are much more clumsy with their non-preferred hand. Also, when the player concentrates on depressing the valves with the left hand, the right hand relaxes, counteracting any potential accumulation of tension.

Slow practice is another example of the repetition of excellence, which is such a sound principle in learning. This can be generalized as follows: every time we have a passage that we struggle with, we can simply change it into something we *can* play. If something is too high, we can play it down an octave or transpose it to a lower key. In this easier register, we should find an improved sound quality and ease of playing, which we can then transfer to the original key. Similarly, if a passage is hard to play with the intended articulation, we can play it legato, study the ease of playing this way, and transfer it to our articulated playing. Or, if the task is to play at an extreme dynamic level, we can establish the desired quality at a normal dynamic, and transfer it to the extreme, whether fortiss(iss)imo or pianiss(iss)imo.

## The Flow Zone

Practicing by repeating excellence—thereby strengthening the neural circuits with myelin, ensuring speedy communication and the sending of precisely timed signals to the muscles for optimal performance—sounds persuasive, as it is a comfortable way of spending a day of practice: repeat beautiful sounds, and enjoy the ease of it. Unfortunately, however, this cannot be the full story, as this strategy merely reinforces great playing in musical passages or technical aspects that the student has already mastered. By contrast, the goal of an ambitious player is constantly to improve his level of performance, and master technical skills or means of musical expression that were not previously within his grasp. Just repeating things we can already play with ease puts us in the comfort zone, where we can easily slip into boredom. Our minds may begin to wander, and we find ourselves thinking about other things: what to have for dinner, I wonder who is on Facebook now, what's on TV tonight, and so on. Mindless practice—simply keeping the movements going, but with little awareness, until we make a mistake and maybe wake up—may not be harmful, but it is certainly an unproductive way of spending our time.

At the opposite end of the spectrum, we have the panic zone, where the music we are playing is beyond our ability. The technical demands are so high that we tense our muscles unnecessarily and counterproductively; we make a lot of mistakes and keep repeating them, thereby "learning" the mistakes, and risking making them permanent. Ambitious students, sometimes with the misguided encouragement of their teachers, often spend too much time in the panic zone, attempting to play music that is beyond their ability, and thereby reinforcing bad habits. This gives the student lots of experience of failing, which—especially when it happens on stage—can be traumatic for a young musician, sapping her self-confidence. It is the duty of the skilled teacher to find repertoire that matches the student's abilities, so he does not waste his time in the comfort zone, repeating the same level of competence and not stretching his skill level, but is also not constantly experiencing failure in the panic zone.

Between the zones of comfort and panic, we have the flow zone, also referred to as the "sweet spot", or the learning zone. Here, the challenge is sufficiently great to demand concentration and focus, but not so high as to cause great anxiety, stress and undesired muscle tension. We are stretching ourselves, reaching for the solution, but we are not overwhelmed by the complexity of the task at hand. In Figure 4, we can think of the challenges as any of the technical demands of brass playing, such as pitch range, dynamic range, speed or stamina.

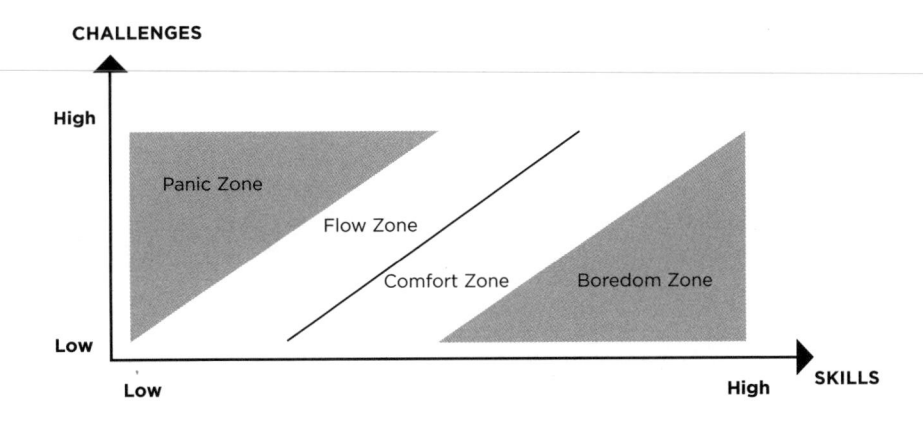

**Figure 4.** The flow zone is above the comfort zone and below the panic zone.

The Hungarian psychologist Mihály Csíkszentmihályi[46] described "flow"

---

46  Csíkszentmihályi, Mihály. *Flow: The Psychology of Optimal Experience* (Harper and Row, 1990).

as a state of mind in which a person is concentrated, and completely immersed in whatever activity he or she is engaged in. In this state, only the task at hand matters, and everyday troubles and worries are simply not present. Performing the activity this way is a fulfilling experience, which comes close to true happiness. Musicians love this mental state, of being engrossed in the process of music making, rather than the outcome; and attaining it is often the pure motivation for practice.[47]

## Deliberate practice

In his groundbreaking book *The Talent Code*[48], Daniel Coyle describes a similar zone for optimal practice, which he calls "deep practice". Another name for the same phenomenon is "deliberate practice". According to Coyle, this state is optimal for learning, as myelin is produced at a higher rate when spending time in this mode.

Coyle describes widely varying areas of expert performance— ranging from soccer and tennis to chess and string playing—in which success has come from deep practice, sustained over many years. The idea that developing expertise in any field requires putting in many hours of practice has recently been popularized as the "10,000-hour rule"[49], which states that it takes at least 10,000 hours of deliberate practice to become expert at anything. A quick calculation translates this to almost three hours of concentrated, focused practice every day for ten years, but in many cases this is a very optimistic estimate. We certainly know expert brass musicians who practiced quite a bit more than this to get to their level.

Coyle bases his conclusions on the work of one of the world's leading psychologists in the field of expertise, the Swede Anders Ericsson. In

---

47  Sterner, Thomas M. *The Practicing Mind: Developing Focus and Discipline in Your Life* (New World Library, 2012).
48  Coyle, Daniel. *The Talent Code* (Arrow Books, 2010).
49  Gladwell, M. *Outliers: The Story of Success* (Little, Brown and Co., 2008). Gladwell based his formulation of the 10,000-hour rule on studies of expertise, including seminal work by the psychologist Anders Ericsson and colleagues (see below). But the idea of a "magic number" for true expertise has been strongly refuted by Ericsson, who argues that there are significant differences among individuals in the amount of practice required to reach a very high level (Ericsson & Pool, cited below).

one study[50], Ericsson and colleagues collected data about practice habits from violinists at the *Hochschule der Künste*—today, the *Universität der Künste* or University of the Arts, in Berlin—and from two orchestras, the Berlin Philharmonic and the Radio Symphony Orchestra of Berlin. The results showed that the individuals who spent the most time practicing in their childhood and adolescent years became the best violinists. It became clear to Ericsson that expert musical performance is not the product of innate talent, present at birth, but instead develops over a decade or more of deliberate practice.

So what does deliberate practice look like?

Deliberate practice takes place outside the comfort zone, and requires the student to try things just beyond his abilities, with close to maximal effort, which is not necessarily enjoyable. It has specific goals, rather than being aimed at some vague general improvement. Deliberate practice requires the student's full attention and concentration, and involves some kind of feedback to monitor progress. The feedback can at first be aided by input from a teacher, and then be taken over by the student himself. As the student engages in deliberate practice, his mental representation of the desired outcome improves in efficiency and detail, which in turn helps him to monitor his progress.[51]

The opposite of deliberate practice is mindless practice. A student engaging in mindless practice may play through a passage until she makes a mistake, stop and fix the mistake, and then move on until the next mistake happens. Deliberate practice also involves making and fixing mistakes, but with full attention, an analytical approach to problem-solving, and a focus on clear attainable goals.

More specifically, for the practicing musician, deliberate practice could look something like this. First, divide the piece you want to work on

---

50   Ericsson, Anders et al. The role of deliberate practice in the acquisition of expert performance. *Psychological Review* **100**, 363-406 (1993).
51   Ericsson, Anders & Pool, Robert. *Peak: Secrets from the New Science of Expertise* (Houghton Mifflin Harcourt, 2016).

(whether solo, etude or excerpt) into short passages. Then, for each passage:

1. Have a clear goal: how do I want this passage to sound?
2. Play it: take a chance and go for it.
3. Evaluate the result: did it sound the way I wanted it to?
4. What do I need to change to reach the goal?
5. Go through steps 2–4 again.

For the brass player, steps 1–4 could be like this:

1. Look at the music and form a clear aural image of the passage, including pitch, rhythm, dynamics and articulation.
2. Play the passage and really go for it. Don't hold back or try to avoid mistakes, but take chances.
3. If you can remember how you sounded, that's great. Otherwise, or in addition, you can record yourself playing in step 2. This will allow you to listen to your playing without simultaneously being engaged in it. Try to be objective when listening to a recording, and focus on the specific aspects of your playing that you are trying to improve.
4. Be analytical here; focus on specific problems, and consider possible solutions.

Questions that you might ask yourself in steps 3 and 4 include, but are not limited to:

Where was my mind during the playing? Did it wander around, worrying about upcoming difficulties, or analyzing previous phrases? Was my concentration "in the moment"? Was I completely engrossed in mentally singing while playing, clearly hearing in my mind what I wanted to come out of the bell? Did I think in subphrases, grouping notes together, or was I just playing mindlessly?

Did I play with an unforced, free sound or did it sound tense? If it was not my best, freest sound, what could the reason be? Did I take a full, relaxed breath, and did I release it immediately, or with hesitation?

Did my abdominal region come in when I was blowing, or did I keep a downward-contracted diaphragm? Was my air constricted in any way—for example, by too-tense lips or a too-high tongue? Did my throat close?

Was my playing rhythmical? Rushing, dragging?

Was my articulation clear? What do I need to change to make it clearer? Shorter consonants, faster air releases? If the articulation was too clear, how can I soften it?

Did I like the vibrato? Did it serve the music well? Was it too slow, too fast or too wide?

How was my intonation? Were any specific notes too sharp or too flat?

Did I follow the dynamics on the page? Do I need to exaggerate more?

How did it feel? Did I expend too much effort? Could I change anything to make it feel easier?

Was I splitting too many notes? If so, can I sing the passage perfectly, in tune and in time? Can I play it in tune on the mouthpiece?

Was my playing as expressive as I would like? What do I have to change, to be able to express what I want?

Deep practice is not just a relaxed pastime, having fun with the instrument. It involves a bit of struggle, and can be mentally exhausting. The key is to have realistic challenges and goals that are attainable: not to be mired in routine boredom, but also not making yourself tense and stressed, by attempting to reach targets that are too challenging.

## Structuring practice time

Teachers often have strong ideas about the best way to structure practice time: some schools of thought prescribe a precise order in which warm-ups, exercises, etudes and orchestral and solo repertoire should be undertaken during the practice day, whereas others can be more relaxed and even anarchic in their approach. Recent research in the field of educational psychology has yielded results that may dramatically change the way brass players arrange their practice time.

## *Blocked practice*

One common way of organizing the practice day—called "blocked" practice—groups the different tasks that need to be addressed into blocks, with each block devoted to one of the tasks. This seems like a very orderly and organized way of practicing; I arranged my practice in this way for decades, and from conversations that I have had at masterclasses, it seems to be the organizing principle used most often by students and teachers around the world.

A blocked practice schedule for a serious trumpet student could look like this:

1. Breathing exercises. 20 minutes
2. Cichowicz Long Tone Studies. 20 minutes
3. Clarke studies no. 1, 2, 3, etc.. Each one can be repeated with single and multiple tonguing. 20 minutes
4. Break
5. Flex-studies, such as Collins, Bai Lin, Irons. 20 minutes
6. Bel canto studies, such as Concone, Bordogni or "The Russian Studies". 20 minutes
7. Etudes, such as Charlier. 20 minutes
8. Break
9. Solo piece, such as Haydn, Enesco, etc.. 30 minutes
10. Orchestral excerpts. 30 minutes

## *Random practice*

An alternative to blocked practice seems at first to be its opposite: messy, out of order and disorganized. In this scheme, different tasks are spread over the day, with the student working on each one for only a short time before proceeding to the next. After having spent a few minutes successively on each task, the student then starts the sequence again from the beginning. In this way, there can be as many repetitions of, and time spent on, each task, exercise or musical passage as in blocked practice, but the work on each task is fragmented; no task is ever rehearsed for more than a few minutes before the student moves on to something else. Even the name of this scheme—random practice—sounds dubious for the ambitious student. It is sometimes referred to, perhaps more aptly, as distributed or interleaved practice.

Random practice could look like this, with this example assuming that the player has already warmed up:

1. Clarke no. 1. 5 minutes
2. Flex study no. 1. 5 minutes
3. Bel canto studies. 5 minutes
4. Etude such as Charlier, first third. 5 minutes
5. Solo piece, middle section. 5 minutes
6. Orchestral excerpt no. 1. 5 minutes

1. Clarke no. 2, legato and tongued. 5 minutes
2. Flex study no. 2. 5 minutes
3. Bel canto studies. 5 minutes
4. Etude such as Charlier, last third. 5 minutes
5. Solo piece, beginning. 5 minutes
6. Orchestral excerpt no. 2. 5 minutes

1. Clarke no. 3, legato and multiple-tongued. 5 minutes
2. Flex study no. 3. 5 minutes
3. Bel canto studies. 5 minutes
4. Etude such as Charlier, middle third. 5 minutes
5. Solo piece, ending. 5 minutes
6. Orchestral excerpt no. 3. 5 minutes

And so on.......

The number of minutes suggested is not important; what matters is that not too much time is spent on each task before moving on to the next.

Random practice may seem messy, but if we look a bit closer we can see that it has a structure, and in fact takes more planning than blocked practice.

A simple way to carry out random practice is to have all the music on the stand, work on one exercise or piece for some minutes, then put it behind the other pieces, work on the next item for a few minutes, put it behind the others, and so on. At some point you are back to the first item, and can start the rotation again with variations, as outlined above.

But why should it matter how you organize your practice? Psychological research says that the two organizational schemes have very different effects on skill acquisition. Blocked practice makes you play better at the time you are doing it. Spending half an hour on one task makes you much better at that task during that half-hour. So, when we do flex studies for a while, it feels great because we get better at it; the task gets easier while we are doing it.

When it comes to long-term learning, however, whether the aim is to learn a motor skill or an academic subject, repeated studies have shown[52] that random practice is much more effective than blocked practice. In a study of baseball players, for example, hitting ability improved by 57% after six weeks of random practice, but by only 25% after the same amount of blocked practice.[53] In another study, mathematics students practiced solving problems over a two-week period, and were then tested in the third week. Although the blocked-practice group outperformed the random-practice group during the two weeks of practice (89% accuracy for blocked versus 60% for random), when tested in week 3, the positions were reversed: 20% accuracy for the blocked group versus 63% for the random-practicers.[54]

One simple explanation for these results could be boredom. Doing the same types of exercise in the same order every day might be a pleasant ritual, but its routine nature can easily lull the student into a comfortable, inattentive state, which is not conducive to long-term learning.

---

52  Shea, John B. & Morgan, Robyn L. Contextual interference effects on the acquisition, retention, and transfer of a motor skill. *Journal of Experimental Psychology: Human Learning and Memory* **5**, 179-187 (1979).
53  Hall, Kellie G. et al. Contextual interference effects with skilled baseball players. *Perceptual and Motor Skills* **78**, 835-841 (1994).
54  Rohrer, Doug & Taylor, Kelli. The shuffling of mathematics problems improves learning. *Instructional Science* **35**, 481-498 (2007).

Psychologists use the term "habituation"[55] to describe what happens when we repeat things many times and stop paying attention. At the beginning of each practice block, we need to pay attention, but then, as we repeat the same things many times, we do not have to think so much about what we are doing. Hence, our practice tends to become automatic, with only limited cognitive involvement. The more we engage the deeper cognitive workings of the brain, the stronger its retention will be, so having to restart the process of learning each task again and again, after having done other interleaved tasks, solidifies the learning over the long term.

Another advantage of random practice is that it is much closer to what we experience in musical performance. When we play real music, we rarely encounter the same technical challenge—whether it be triple tonguing, high notes or soft playing—over and over again. Instead, music is a constantly changing mix of many elements, requiring us to be flexible, and able to meet whatever challenges come our way.

Blocked practice may give us the illusion of having mastered a given task, by giving us a chance to warm up into it, and repeat it many times. But in an audition or a concert, we have only one opportunity to get something right. It is cruel, but random practice prepares us much better for this challenge.

### *Varied practice*
In 1978, groups of 8-year-olds and 12-year-olds practiced throwing beanbags into buckets for 12 weeks, as part of an investigation of the efficiency of different kinds of practice.[56] In each age group, half of the children practiced throwing the beanbags into a bucket placed 3 feet away, and the other half threw them into buckets placed 2 and 4 feet away. After the 12 weeks of practice, all of the children were tested at throwing the beanbags into the bucket 3 feet away. Following the logic of "what we repeat we get better at", one would intuitively guess that the

---

55 Rankin, Catharine H. et al. Habituation revisited: an updated and revised description of the behavioral characteristics of habituation. *Neurobiology of Learning and Memory* **92**, 135–138 (2009).
56 Kerr, Robert & Booth, Bernard. Specific and varied practice of motor skill. *Perceptual and Motor Skills* **46**, 395-401 (1978).

groups who had practiced only throwing the beanbags 3 feet would be better at this task. The results showed the opposite: the groups who had varied their practice performed significantly better than those who had done constant or specific practice.

These findings favoring varied practice have found support, and a possible explanation, more recently in research using a technique called transcranial magnetic stimulation to interfere with motor-skill retention in two different parts of the brain.[57] The results of this study showed that the learning from varied practice, which is more cognitively challenging than constant practice, appears to be consolidated in a part of the brain associated with the more difficult process of learning higher-order motor skills. Conversely, the learning from constant practice seemed to be consolidated in a brain region that is used to control simpler motor skills.[58] In other words, varied practice involves more brainpower in encoding learning, and creates a richer neural representation of the task, which can be applied more broadly.

When practicing standard audition pieces or excerpts, we often have a clear goal of an ideal version that we are trying to reach. This could be a famous recording by a great player, or a particular accepted way to play certain excerpts. When trying to reach this clear goal, we are engaging in constant practice, analogous to throwing the bean bags into just one bucket. From what we have just learned, it would seem more advantageous to practice our standard repertoire in a wide variety of ways. How many different ways can we think of playing a well known passage?

Some suggestions for varied practice include:

Change the tempo, the dynamics, and the rhythm, and try different articulations and keys.

---

[57] Kantak, Shailesh S. et al. Neural substrates of motor memory consolidation depend on practice structure. *Nature Neuroscience* **13**, 923–925 (2010).
[58] Brown, Peter C., Roediger III, Henry L. & McDaniel, Mark A. *Make It Stick: The Science of Successful Learning* (Belknap Press, 2014).

Try to play the passage as your three favorite players of your own instrument would play it. Alternatively, how would Maria Callas sing it? How would it sound on a violin, played by three different violinists?

Change equipment: play the same music on different mouthpieces, or differently tuned instruments. For example, when preparing the Haydn on B-flat trumpet, play it on piccolo trumpet, C-trumpet, flugelhorn, etc..

Play in different rooms: with good acoustics, bad acoustics, resonant and dry.

Practice the music with different moods: happy, sad, enthusiastic, like a national anthem, seductively, angry, joyful, etc..

In short, you can find endless new ways to play music that may have become stale, after you have attempted to play it in one particular way for years. Practicing this way is not only more fun, but, as we have seen, it does a better job of engaging the brain, so that playing the music in that one ideal way, to which you have aspired for a long time, will soon come within your reach.

## Learning styles

Another recent educational trend that has found its way into music education is a focus on individual learning styles. According to this view, learners can be classified according to their preferences for, or strengths in, different ways of acquiring and processing information.[59] The performance coach Don Greene lists the following five learning styles:

1. Visual
2. Auditory
3. Kinesthetic
4. Cognitive
5. Trial and experience

---

59  Barbe, Walter B. & Milone Jr, Michael N. What we know about modality strengths. *Educational Leadership* **38**, 378–380 (1981).

In the musical context, visual and auditory learning occur when we watch and listen to a teacher demonstrating playing. Kinesthetic learning happens when we register the sensation of specific actions in our muscles. Cognitive learning takes place when someone explains to us how to do something; and trial-and-experience describes the process of trying something repeatedly, until we succeed.[60]

According to the general view of learning styles, all learners will use all of these modes to some extent, but with individual preferences and strengths. Most people will have one or two dominant styles that they prefer, and identifying these enables a teacher to deliver information in the most efficient manner for each student. Similarly, a student who knows which learning mode is dominant for him will be able to find the best way to learn something, whether it be a new technique, or new repertoire.[61]

Although it may make intuitive sense to stick with one's dominant learning mode, there is also a hidden potential in exploring modes that are not the strongest or most preferred. For example, when we find ourselves on a plateau—whether in our general playing, or with a particular piece—using one or more of the other modes can provide the challenge needed to engage parts of the brain that can help with deeper learning, as we discussed above in the context of varied practice.

Brass players, in particular, will benefit from cultivating certain learning styles, regardless of the preferences of the individual player. Brass instruments, unlike strings or piano, do not lend themselves to visual learning, as most of the movements responsible for tone production occur invisibly, inside the player. Similarly, much of a brass player's technique is beyond conscious cognitive awareness when playing. Learning by trial and

---

60    Greene, Don. *11 Strategies for Audition and Performance Success* (2012). Workbook, available at http://psi.dongreene.com/wp-content/uploads/11Strategies.pdf.
61    Despite the widespread use and popularity of learning styles in educational approaches in many fields, an evaluation of the learning-styles literature did not find evidence for the practical utility of classifying students by their learning styles. Nevertheless, they acknowledge that it would be premature to dismiss the general approach, as there is a lack of methodologically sound studies in this field. Pashler, Harold et al. Learning styles: concepts and evidence. *Psychological Science in the Public Interest* 9, 105-119 (2009).

experience brings the risk of "practicing mistakes"; it can also be quite time-consuming, exposing the player to the dangers of over-practice, such as over-tiring or damaging the lips.

By contrast, auditory and kinesthetic learning have great potential for all brass players. Listening to our sound is the surest guide to whether we are using good technique; and, as discussed earlier, listening to and imitating great players is an efficient way to learn. Sensing what our muscles are doing helps us to distinguish between effortful, muscular playing and easy, free, efficient playing, involving minimal effort. Once again, we come back to the essentials of Song and Wind.

## Mental practice

By now it should be clear that learning to master a musical instrument has more to do with programming the brain than with building muscles, or mindlessly repeating exercises. Consistent with this is the growing popularity of mental practice.

A classic study performed by Alvaro Pascual-Leone[62] enrolled groups of people who had never played a musical instrument in a five-day training period. One group practiced a five-finger exercise for two hours a day, while another group just imagined playing the same exercise—sitting at the keyboard, visualizing the movements, but with no physical practice. After each practice session, all of the subjects were tested on their playing of the exercise; in addition, transcranial magnetic stimulation (TMS) was used to map the part of their brains responsible for the relevant finger movements. There was also a control group, who did not do any practice, but were tested each day.

As expected, the control group showed no significant improvement over the five days. The group that showed the greatest improvement was the physical-practice group, followed by the mental-practice group, who by day 5 had reached the competence level of the physical group at

---

62  Pascual-Leone, Alvaro. The brain that plays music and is changed by it. *Annals of the New York Academy of Sciences* **930**, 315-329 (2001).

day 3, just from imagining playing. At the end of day 5, the researchers let the mental group practice physically for just 5 minutes, after which they performed as well as the physical group! It seems, therefore, that a combination of physical and mental practice must be ideal. One might think that this would pertain only to beginners, but a similar study performed with 16 advanced pianists (all of whom had played the piano for at least 15 years) yielded similar results: after 30 minutes of practice, the physical group had learned more music and made fewer errors than the mental group; but after 10 more minutes, during which time both groups could do physical practice, the mental group scored almost as well as the physical group.[63][64]

Interestingly, in the earlier study by Pascual-Leone, both the physical and the mental groups exhibited changes in their brains, as revealed by the TMS mapping. So just *thinking* about playing changes the brain *physically*.

This offers great possibilities for brass players, many of whom find that the amount of physical practice they can do in a day is limited by their lip muscles becoming tired, or even bruised. In today's stressful world, we see more and more players suffering from focal dystonia, and other consequences of overuse. Beyond this benefit, mental practice also gives us opportunities to make good use of activities that might otherwise be a waste of time, such as travelling or standing in line.

Mental practice is not just thinking loosely about playing, but demands real focus. There can be a lot to imagine: the sound in all of its aspects (timbre, dynamics, articulations, phrasing, vibrato); the fingers depressing the valves; the feeling of the lips when they are vibrating optimally, or the tongue when it is moving freely; the wind at the lips, and the feeling of the respiratory

---

63   Bernardi, Nicolò Francesco et al. Mental practice in music memorization: an ecological-empirical study. *Music Perception* **30**, 275–290 (2013).
64   Perhaps surprisingly, the power of mental practice extends beyond the development of complex motor skills, such as those involved in playing a musical instrument, to strength training. A study comparing the effects of physical and mental practice in high-intensity resistance training showed strength gains of 5.1% in a group doing the training physically, as compared with 3.0–4.2% gains for groups spending from 75% to 25% of their training purely in their heads, without contracting their muscles. [Reiser, Mathias et al. Frontiers in Psychology 2, 194 (2011).]

muscles; and so forth. With such a vivid picture, mental practice can be very effective; in fact, it can be more effective than physical practice, because, in the mind, one's playing can be 100% perfect, 100% ideal and 100% easy—an outcome that is achieved only rarely in the real, physical world. In mental practice, one never has to practice mistakes.

Some performers also use visualization to prepare for performances, as a way of getting the brain accustomed to the situation in advance. By imagining an audition or concert repeatedly in calm circumstances, the performer can program the mind to function well under pressure, because when the day comes, the event will seem familiar, from all the mental rehearsal.

Another, particularly effective, use of mental practice is to combine vivid mental rehearsal with different learning styles. Thus, a student might mentally run through a particular passage three times, using her three most dominant learning styles. When the student returns to the instrument after these three mental rehearsals, the improvement in the certainty and expressiveness of the playing can be dramatic.

We have seen that learning and performance can be enhanced by combining real, physical practice with vividly imagined mental practice, even when most of the repetitions are done mentally. Getting into the habit of imagining all aspects of playing very strongly in the mind, before engaging in the physical execution, can also be a very effective way of building confidence in the performer, as the success rate of his physical playing will be much higher after many perfect mental rehearsals, than after many physical repetitions of trial and error.

## Brain waves and performance

Another phenomenon that has caught the attention of the athletic world for quite a while, and where coaches in music performance may also see potential benefit for learning and peak performance, is that of neural oscillations, popularly known as brain waves.[65] [66] When groups of neurons in our brains communicate with each other, the synchronized electrical pulses produce brain waves. These brain waves can be recorded and measured using sensors placed on the scalp, in a technique called electroencephalography (EEG). With the help of this tool, brain waves have been classified into different types, according to their characteristic frequencies, with each type reflecting a different state, or activity, of the brain. All wave types are always present in the living brain, but some will dominate over others, depending on our mental state. The main types relevant to our purpose are alpha, beta, delta and theta waves.

Delta waves have the slowest oscillation frequencies[67], and are characteristic of deep sleep. The next, in order of frequency, are theta waves; these are also prominent in sleep, and when we are deeply relaxed, such as while we are daydreaming, meditating or undergoing hypnosis.[68] Alpha waves, which dominate when we are relaxed and mentally flexible, are very interesting for our purpose, as they seem suited for peak performance. In particular, the virtues that we have discussed above as being characteristic of Self 2, and "right brain" activity, appear to be related to alpha waves, and to some degree theta waves.

Activities that are known to promote alpha-wave activity include meditation, guided imagery, visualization and relaxation exercises, to name just a few. We will discuss below how performers can get into this state on demand, and when under pressure.

Beta waves are characteristic of waking consciousness, and are dominant when we are alert and active. This state is great for analyzing, problem solving, writing and reading books about embouchures, and other activities associated with Self 1 and "left brain" thinking. We can get into this mode when we are stressed: excessive beta activity in the frontal

---

65 Loehr, James E. *The New Toughness Training for Sports* (Plume, 1995).
66 Greene, D. *Performance Success* (Routledge. 2002).
67 https://en.wikipedia.org/wiki/Electroencephalography
68 Sabourin, M. E. et al. EEG correlates of hypnotic susceptibility and hypnotic trance: spectral analysis and coherence. *International Journal of Psychophysiology* **10**, 125-142 (1990).

lobes has been linked to anxiety and post-traumatic stress disorder[69]. We typically experience beta activity as a lot of internal chatter and noise, which is detrimental to great performance.

There have been several studies of the role played by brain waves in peak performance in sports, [70][71][72] and this connection has also recently been studied in musicians.

One study[73] involving conservatory students (from the Royal College of Music in London) divided subjects into several groups, to study the effect of different brain-training methods. Three of the groups were taught to use EEG-neurofeedback: one to induce alpha and theta waves, a second to encourage beta waves, and a third to promote another type of higher-frequency wave called sensorimotor rhythm. A fourth group used mental skills training, derived from sports psychology; a fifth did physical exercise; and a sixth worked with the Alexander Technique[74]. Before and after the training period, which lasted 6–8 weeks, the subjects performed two pieces, which were judged by external expert musicians. Interestingly, only the group trained to boost their alpha and theta waves demonstrated improved musical performance. As can be seen in Figure 5, this improvement was evident in the overall quality, musical understanding, stylistic accuracy and interpretative imagination—or, as one of the

---

69    Begic, D. et al. Electroencephalographic comparison of veterans with combat-related post-traumatic stress disorder and healthy subjects. *International Journal of Psychophysiology* **40**, 167-172 (2001).
70    Shelley-Tremblay, John F. et al. Changes in EEG laterality index effects of social inhibition on putting in novice golfers. *Journal of Sport Behavior* **29**, 353-373 (2006).
71    Landers, D. M. et al. Effects of learning on electroencephalographic and electrocardiographic patterns in novice archers. *International Journal of Sport Psychology* **25**, 313-330 (1994).
72    Baumeister, J. et al. Cortical activity of skilled performance in a complex sports related motor task. *European Journal of Applied Physiology* **104**, 625-631 (2008).
73    Egner, Tobias & Gruzelier, John H. Ecological validity of neurofeedback: modulation of slow wave EEG enhances musical performance. *NeuroReport* **14**, 1221-1224 (2003).
74    The Alexander Technique is a system of kinesthetic education aimed at avoiding excessive postural tension, and is well known for being efficient in postural retraining and somatic stress reduction.

researchers wrote,[75] "essentially the artistic domain of performance." The improvements were significant—equivalent to a difference of two class grades, with some students improving their scores by as much as 50%.

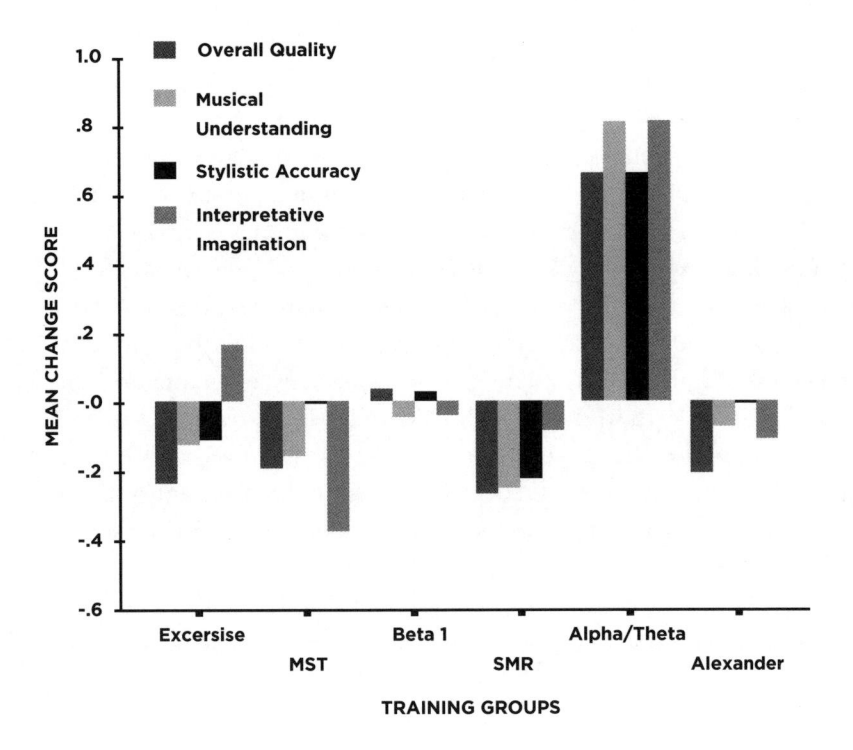

**Figure 5.** This graph, reproduced from Gruzelier (2009), shows how only the group trained to induce alpha/theta brain waves succeeded in improving the quality of their musical performance, in a comparison with other training methods that only reduced performance anxiety.

Interestingly, all of the interventions reduced performance anxiety, but the artistic enhancement in the alpha/theta group could not be attributed solely to stress reduction. Instead, it seemed that the alpha/theta training had brought the students into a mode beyond mere relaxation, and in the

---

75   Gruzelier, John. A theory of alpha/theta neurofeedback, creative performance enhancement, long distance functional connectivity and psychological integration. *Cognitive Processing* **10**, *Issue 1 Supplement,* 101-109 (2009).

direction of more creative, peak performance.[76] The training involved performing EEG-neurofeedback while relaxing, with eyes closed and listening to pleasant sounds, such as the gentle crashing of waves on a beach or the babbling of a brook. The feedback protocol was designed so that the subjects maximized the ratio of theta to alpha waves.[77]

## *Centering*

In the competitive environment of today's classical music profession, we could all benefit from the ability to shift on demand, in performance situations, from a stressed, highly analytical mode involving beta waves to the alpha/theta state just described. The legendary performance psychologist Don Greene has had great success helping performers in all spheres (including divers, race-car drivers, golfers, opera singers, instrumentalists, SWAT-officers and Wall Street brokers) to do just this. Central to his method of getting performers into peak performance mode is a process known as "centering", which he learned from his mentor, Robert Nideffer. In developing this technique, Nideffer was inspired by the martial art of aikido, which he had studied in Japan. Centering is a very efficient way of regulating energy, not least because it is not designed to completely eliminate or fight adrenaline, but to get it partially under control and use it positively to enhance our performance. The centering

---

76   John Gruzelier (*op. cit.*) writes, "In an interpretative phenomenological analysis based on a structured interview with a subgroup of the music students, Edge and Lancaster (2004) found that states achieved whilst carrying out A/T neurofeedback were described as similar but not the same as those experienced when performing or playing music: 'They're kind of non-identical twins'. Subsequently a student who has gone on to have an international career as one of a piano duo, and who continued to be adept at achieving a crossover state, wrote 'During the training sessions I feel extremely relaxed and as though my mind is able to freely glide with my creative ideas bringing a new kind of spontaneity and energy to my thought processes…this gives me the opportunity to explore other areas of creativity that were previously unavailable to me as I'm free from the physical act of playing the piano whilst mentally being in the state of a performance. It's an extremely satisfying state to be in as it's almost as though I've been introduced to thinking of nothing, which then takes me to a place where creative possibilities seem boundless'."

77   EEG equipment used to be quite costly, but today neurofeedback systems are available for affordable prices, and are easy to use. Muse ("the brain sensing headband") is a product that is designed to provide feedback during meditation, and while performing other tasks. Professional golfers have started to use Muse to help in training their focus and concentration, as preparation for peak performance. www.choosemuse.com

process also involves breathing and focusing, and is especially beneficial for brass players as it includes preparatory steps that are particularly essential for us.

The process[78] includes seven steps that have to be learned and memorized, which facilitate the shift from a stressed mode towards one with more alpha waves. At first, it may take one to two minutes to complete the sequence of steps, but after three weeks of daily training, you will be able to attain the optimal mode in about ten seconds.

The seven steps are:

1. Form a clear intention
2. Pick a focal point
3. Breathe mindfully
4. Relax key muscles
5. Find your center
6. Imagine the optimal sound and feel of the opening bar
7. Direct the energy to the focal point

There are profound reasons for each step:

1. *Form a clear intention.*
   Having a clear intention for what you are going to play acts like a positive psychological cue. This will usually work best if you use process-oriented, positive words, instead of words related to the outcome, or negative expressions. Phrases such as, "let go of the first notes", "play it on the wind", "sing in your mind", "clear tonguing" and "beautiful sounds" will usually work better than "play perfectly" or "don't miss any notes".
2. *Pick a focal point.*
   Try to look somewhere in front of you, below eye level. This could be the music you are going to play or, if you are playing from memory, somewhere in the hall. Having somewhere to rest your eyes will

---

[78]  Centering can be learned from instructional videos with Don Greene, available for purchase at dongreene.com.

make you feel and look calmer than looking up or having shifty eyes. Alternatively, close your eyes if possible, as this has been shown to increase the amplitude of alpha waves.

3. *Breathe mindfully.*

    Take full, relaxed breaths: in through the nose, and out through the mouth. Taking air through the nose will usually induce deep diaphragmatic breathing. However, most brass players can do this when breathing through the mouth; you can accordingly decide to take a good WOH-breath (discussed in the chapter on breathing) as an alternative to inhaling through the nose. Apart from the obvious benefits for wind players of taking full breaths, deep breathing also has a calming effect, as it increases alpha and theta waves,[79] and lowers blood pressure.[80]

4. *Relax key muscles.*

    Scan the most important muscle groups for your instrument progressively as you breathe in, and relax them as you breathe out. Often we do not notice, as we are practicing or performing, how much we are tensing muscle groups essential to playing. By going through them one by one, we can be sure to relax them. Start with face, lips, tongue and jaw; then go on to throat and neck, shoulders, arms and breathing muscles. This will set you up for a relaxed approach to playing.

5. *Find your center.*

    This is located approximately 5 centimeters below the navel, and 5 centimeters into the body. In Japanese and Chinese traditions of martial arts, the center is involved in the energy flow known as ki, chi or qi. For the Western mind, it might be useful to think of it as the body's center of gravity. We can also think of it as being involved in diaphragmatic breathing. Even though the diaphragm is not that low in the human body, deep breathing will feel very low because of the displacement of the abdominal organs. Finally, focusing internally on this part of the body as you search for your center may trigger more

---

[79] Rojviroj, Wanee et al. Study of brain activity analysis of deep breathing. Preprint available at http://www.mfu.ac.th/school/anti-aging/File_PDF/research_inter/P2557_21.pdf.

[80] Lee, John S. et al. Effects of diaphragmatic breathing on ambulatory blood pressure and heart rate. *Biomedicine & Pharmacotherapy* **57**, 87-91 (2003).

alpha waves.[81]

6. *Imagine the optimal sound and feel of the opening bar.*
   As we have discussed throughout this book, mentally hearing and conceiving the sound of the music you are about to play is essential to successful performance, as it takes you away from trying to control specific muscle groups, and into letting the music happen by trusting Self 2. Adding to this aural image a kinesthetic one of the "feel" of optimal playing helps to program your body to perform as easily as possible.

7. *Direct the energy to the focal point.*
   This is the final step, where you take a breath and let your internal energy move out into the hall. You can think of this figuratively, as feeling the nervous energy and using it positively when playing the first bar. Alternatively, you can think more concretely, of aerodynamic energy coming from a deep diaphragmatic breath and the abdomen's role in the tHO articulation described earlier. You can also connect the release of stored energy with the idea of "loosing the shots" in Zen archery—letting go of your first notes, instead of trying to control them.

*Practicing centering*
You will need to practice centering diligently and attentively, to be able to do it quickly in stressful situations, with optimal effect.

**In the first week**, you should practice it at least seven times a day—ideally, sitting, and without your instrument.

1. *Form a clear intention.* "I am going to practice centering."
2. *Pick a focal point.* Find a point on which to rest the eyes, below eye level.
3. *Breathe mindfully.* Breathe in through the nose and out through the mouth relatively slowly, a few times, until you are starting to feel calmer.
4. *Relax key muscles.* Scan key muscles while breathing in, and let go of

---

[81] Kerr, Catherine E. et al. Mindfulness starts with the body: somatosensory attention and top-down modulation of cortical alpha rhythms in mindfulness meditation. *Frontiers in Human Neuroscience* (13 February 2013). http://dx.doi.org/10.3389/fnhum.2013.00012

tension while breathing out. Include face, lips, tongue, jaw, throat, neck, shoulders, breathing muscles and arms/hands.
5. *Find your center.* Be aware of your center; feel it as you keep breathing.
6. *Imagine the optimal sound and feel of the opening bar.* Hear and feel your first notes very clearly.
7. *Direct the energy to the focal point.* Take a deep breath, gather all your energy in the center, and send it to the focal point with a sigh.

**In the second week**, again, practice at least seven times a day, now sitting or standing with your instrument. Breathe once per step.

1. *Form a clear intention.* Think a process cue, such as "beautiful playing".
2. *Pick a focal point.* Find a point on which to rest the eyes, below eye level.
3. *Breathe mindfully.* Breathe in through the nose, out through the mouth, relatively slowly, once.
4. *Relax key muscles.* Scan key muscles on the in-breath, then release the tension in all of your key muscles in one big sigh.
5. *Find your center.* Be aware of the center; feel it as you breathe in and out.
6. *Imagine the optimal sound and feel of the opening bar.* Hear and feel the opening bar very clearly, while breathing in and out once.
7. *Direct the energy to the focal point.* Bring the instrument into playing position, take a deep breath, gather all your energy in the center, and without hesitation, send the energy, the air and the sound to the focal point.

**In the third week**, practice centering every time you return from a break, or between segments of your practice routine. Now, the entire process is done using only three breaths. Before the first one, form a clear intention and pick a focal point, then:

1. Take a big breath while scanning all key muscles for tension; then release the tension with the breath.
2. Be at your center while breathing in, and imagine the sound and feel of the opening bar while breathing out.

3. Raise the instrument and breathe in while gathering the energy in the center; then let go (play) to the focal point.

Thus, a process that may have originally seemed cumbersome has become, after diligent practice, a streamlined affair lasting only 10–15 seconds. It should be an easy and automatic way of triggering essential functions that are necessary for successful brass performance. The technique can be used during performances, as well as before them; for example, during rests, you can use longer or shorter forms of centering to prepare for your next entrance and stay focused, not letting your mind wander.

After you have become proficient at centering, you can simulate the effects of adrenalin by artificially raising your pulse—for example, by running up and down stairs, or doing wall-sits or push-ups. Then center and play. Pretty soon, you will become used to playing with excess energy that you can regulate with centering, and use positively to enhance your performance.

Performers have different preferences when it comes to assessing the optimal energy level for performing; some like to be calm, while others prefer to be excited. The problem arises when a performer is unable to control his energy level while performing—for example, when someone who needs to be calm to play well keeps finding himself in an agitated state while performing. Such a player can use the simulation training described above to practice playing with higher energy, and also to lower the energy with centering, so the gap between the optimal energy and that of actual performance gets smaller.